# QUICK SKILLS
# Fourth Grade

Carson Dellosa Education
Greensboro, NC

Carson Dellosa Education
PO Box 35665
Greensboro, NC 27425  USA

ISBN  978-1-4838-6826-4

01-261237784

## Language Arts

## Math

## Answer Key

# Say It Short

**Vowels** are the letters **a, e, i, o, u** and sometimes **y**. There are five short vowels: **ă** as in **a**pple, **ĕ** as in **e**gg, **ĭ** as in s**i**ck, **ŏ** as in t**o**p, and **ŭ** as in **u**p.

**Directions:** Complete the exercises using words from the box.

| blend | insist | health | pump | crop |
|-------|--------|--------|------|------|
| fact | pinch | pond | hatch | plug |

1.  Write each word under its vowel sound.

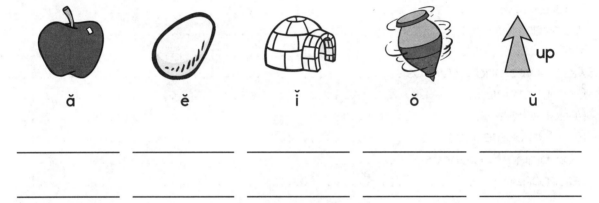

| ă | ĕ | ĭ | ŏ | ŭ |

_____  _____  _____  _____  _____

_____  _____  _____  _____  _____

2.  Complete these sentences, using a word with the vowel sound given. Use each word from the box only once. Not all words will be used.

Here's an interesting (ă) _____ about your (ĕ) _____.

The kids enjoyed fishing in the (ŏ) _____.

They (ĭ) _____ on watching the egg (ă) _____.

(ĕ) _____ in a (ĭ) _____ of salt.

Did you (ŭ) _____ in the lamp?

# Say It Long: a and e

Long **ā** can be spelled **a** as in **apron**, **ai** as in **pail**, **ay** as in **pay**, or **a-e** as in **lake**. Long **ē** can be spelled **ea** as in **real** or **ee** as in **deer**.

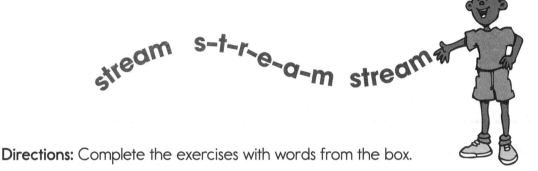

**Directions:** Complete the exercises with words from the box.

| deal | clay | grade | weave | stream |
|------|------|-------|-------|--------|
| pain | tape | sneeze | claim | treat |

1. Write each word in the row with the matching vowel sound.

   ā  _____  _____  _____  _____  _____

   ē  _____  _____  _____  _____  _____

2. Complete each sentence, using a word with the vowel sound given. Use each word from the word box only once. Not all words will be used.

   Everyone in (ā) _____ four ate an ice-cream (ē) _____.

   Every time I (ē) _____, I feel (ā) _____ in my chest.

   When I (ē) _____ with yarn, I put a piece of (ā) _____ on the loose ends so they won't come undone.

   You (ā) _____ you got a good (ē) _____ on your new bike, but I still think you paid too much.

# Say It Long: i and o

Long ī can be spelled **i** as in **wild**, **igh** as in **night**, **i-e** as in **wipe**, or **y** as in **try**. Long ō can be spelled **o** as in **most**, **oa** as in **toast**, **ow** as in **throw**, or **o-e** as in **hope**.

**Directions:** Complete the exercises with words from the box.

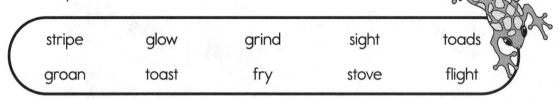

| stripe | glow | grind | sight | toads |
| groan | toast | fry | stove | flight |

1. Write each word from the box with its vowel sound.

ī  _____  _____  _____  _____  _____

ō  _____  _____  _____  _____  _____

2. Complete these sentences, using a word with the given vowel sound. Use each word from the box only once. Not all words will be used.

We will (ī) _____ potatoes on the (ō) _____.

I thought I heard a low (ō) _____, but when I looked, there was

nothing in (ī) _____.

The airplane for our (ī) _____ had a (ī) _____ painted on its side.

Do (ō) _____ live in the water like frogs?

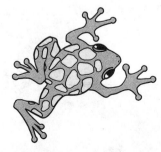

# Say It Long: u

Long ū can be spelled **u-e** as in **cube** or **ew** as in **few**. Some sounds are similar in sound to u but are not true **u** sounds, such as the **oo** in **tooth**, the **o-e** in **move**, and the **ue** in **blue**.

**Directions:** Complete each sentence using a word from the box. Do not use the same word more than once.

| blew | tune | flute | cute | June | glue |

1. Yesterday, the wind _____ so hard it knocked down a tree on our street.

2. My favorite instrument is the _____.

3. The little puppy in the window is so _____.

4. I love _____ because it's so warm, and we get out of school.

5. For that project, you will need scissors, construction paper, and _____.

6. I recognize that song because it has a familiar _____.

Name _____

# Say It with Synonyms

A **synonym** is a word that means the same, or nearly the same, as another word.

**Example: quick** and **fast**

**Directions:** Draw lines to match the words in Column A with their synonyms in Column B.

| Column A | Column B |
|----------|----------|
| plain | unusual |
| career | vocation |
| rare | disappear |
| vanish | greedy |
| beautiful | finish |
| selfish | simple |
| complete | lovely |

**Directions:** Choose a word from Column A or Column B to complete each sentence below.

1. Dad was very excited when he discovered the _____ coin for sale on the display counter.

2. My dog is a real magician; he can _____ into thin air when he sees me getting his bath ready!

3. Many of my classmates joined the discussion about _____ choices we had considered.

4. "You will need to _____ your report on ancient Greece before you sign up for computer time," said Mr. Rastetter.

5. Your _____ painting will be on display in the art show.

# Antonyms All Around

An **antonym** is a word that means the opposite of another word.

**Example: difficult** and **easy**

**Directions:** Choose words from the box to complete the crossword puzzle.

| | | | |
|---|---|---|---|
| friend | vanish | quit | safety |
| liquids | scatter | help | noisy |

**ACROSS:**

2. Opposite of **gather**

3. Opposite of **enemy**

4. Opposite of **prevent**

6. Opposite of **begin**

7. Opposite of **silent**

**DOWN:**

1. Opposite of **appear**

2. Opposite of **danger**

5. Opposite of **solids**

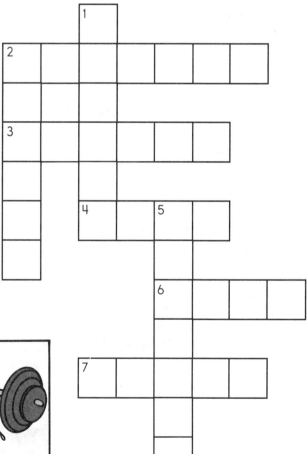

# Hear! Here! Homophones!

**Homophones** are two words that sound the same, have different meanings, and are usually spelled differently.

**Example: write** and **right**

**Directions:** Write the correct homophone in each sentence below.

**weight** — how heavy something is

**wait** — to be patient

**steal** — to take something that doesn't belong to you

**steel** — a heavy metal

**threw** — tossed

**through** — passing between

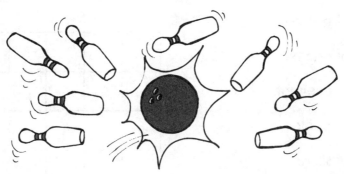

1. The bands marched _____ the streets lined with many cheering people.

2. _____ for me by the flagpole.

3. One of our strict rules at school is: Never _____ from another person.

4. Could you estimate the _____ of this bowling ball?

5. The bleachers have _____ rods on both ends and in the middle.

6. He walked in the door and _____ his jacket down.

# Prefix Pros

A **prefix** is a syllable at the beginning of a word that changes its meaning.

**Directions:** Add a prefix to the beginning of each word in the box to make a word with the meaning given in each sentence below. The first one is done for you.

| PREFIX | MEANING |
|--------|---------|
| bi | two or twice |
| en | to make |
| in | within |
| mis | wrong |
| non | not or without |
| pre | before |
| re | again |
| un | not |

> grown      write      information      large      cycle      sense

1. Antonio's foot hurt because his toenail was (growing within). **ingrown**

2. If you want to see what is in the background, you will have to (make bigger) the photograph. _____

3. I didn't do a very good job on my homework, so I will have to (write it again) it. _____

4. The newspaper article about the event has some (wrong facts). _____

5. I hope I get a (vehicle with two wheels) for my birthday. _____

6. The story he told was complete (words without meaning)! _____

Name _____

# Save the Best for Last

A **suffix** is a syllable at the end of a word that changes its meaning. In most cases, when adding a suffix that begins with a vowel, drop the final **e** of the root word. For example, **fame** becomes **famous**. Also, change a final **y** in the root word to **i** before adding any suffix except **ing**. For example, **silly** becomes **silliness**.

**Directions:** Add a suffix to the end of each word in the box to make a word with the meaning given (in parentheses) in each sentence below. The first one is done for you.

| SUFFIX | MEANING |
|--------|---------|
| ful | full of |
| ity | quality or degree |
| ive | have or tend to be |
| less | without or lacking |
| able | able to be |
| ness | state of |
| ment | act of |
| or | person that does something |
| ward | in the direction of |

| like | thought | pay | thank | act | happy |
|------|---------|-----|-------|-----|-------|

1. Mike was (full of thanks) for a hot meal. _____**thankful**_____

2. I was (without thinking) for forgetting your birthday. _____

3. Tasha is such a (able to be liked) girl! _____

4. Jill's wedding day was one of great (the state of being happy). _____

5. The (person who performs) was very good in the play. _____

6. I have to make a (act of paying) for the stereo I bought. _____

# Come on and Compare

An **analogy** indicates how different items go together or are similar in some way.

**Examples: Petal** is to **flower** as **leaf** is to **tree.**
     **Book** is to **library** as **food** is to **grocery.**

If you study the examples, you will see how the second set of objects is related to the first set. A petal is part of a flower, and a leaf is part of a tree. A book can be found in a library, and food can be found in a grocery store.

**Directions:** Fill in the blanks to complete the analogies. The first one has been done for you.

1. Cup is to saucer as glass is to _____ **coaster** _____.

2. Paris is to France as London is to _____.

3. Clothes are to hangers as _____ are to boxes.

4. California is to _____ as Ohio is to Lake Erie.

5. _____ is to table as blanket is to bed.

6. Pencil is to paper as _____ is to canvas.

7. Cow is to _____ as child is to house.

8. State is to country as _____ is to state.

9. Governor is to state as _____ is to country.

**Directions:** Write three analogies of your own.

_____

_____

_____

Name _____

# Let's Get Cooking!

Sequencing is putting items or events in logical order.

**Directions:** Read the recipe. Then, number the steps in order for making brownies.

Preheat the oven to 350 degrees. Grease an 8-inch square baking dish.

In a mixing bowl, place two squares (2 ounces) of unsweetened chocolate and $\frac{1}{3}$ cup butter. Place the bowl in a pan of hot water and heat it to melt the chocolate and the butter.

When the chocolate is melted, remove the pan from the heat. Add 1 cup sugar and two eggs to the melted chocolate and beat it. Next, stir in $\frac{3}{4}$ cup sifted flour, $\frac{1}{2}$ teaspoon baking powder and $\frac{1}{2}$ teaspoon salt. Finally, mix in $\frac{1}{2}$ cup chopped nuts.

Spread the mixture in the greased baking dish. Bake for 30 to 35 minutes. The brownies are done when a toothpick stuck in the center comes out clean. Let the brownies cool. Cut them into squares.

_____ Stick a toothpick in the center of the brownies to make sure they are done.

_____ Mix in chopped nuts.

_____ Melt chocolate and butter in a mixing bowl over a pan of hot water.

_____ Cool brownies and cut into squares.

_____ Beat in sugar and eggs.

_____ Spread mixture in a baking dish.

_____ Stir in flour, baking powder and salt.

_____ Bake for 30 to 35 minutes.

_____ Turn oven to 350 degrees and grease pan.

# Right on Track

**Directions:** Below is part of a schedule for trains leaving New York City for cities all around the country. Use the schedule to answer the questions.

| Destination | Train Number | Departure Time | Arrival Time |
| --- | --- | --- | --- |
| Birmingham | 958 | 9:00 a.m. | 12:31 a.m. |
| Boston | 611 | 7:15 a.m. | 4:30 p.m. |
| Cambridge | 398 | 8:15 a.m. | 1:14 p.m. |
| Cincinnati | 242 | 5:00 a.m. | 7:25 p.m. |
| Detroit | 415 | 1:45 p.m. | 4:40 a.m. |
| Evansville | 623 | 3:00 p.m. | 8:28 a.m. |

1. What is the number of the train that leaves latest in the day? _____

2. What city is the destination for train number 623? _____

3. What time does the train for Boston leave New York? _____

4. What time does train number 415 arrive in Detroit? _____

5. What is the destination of the train that leaves earliest

   in the day? _____

# That's a Fact!

**Facts** are statements or events that have happened and can be proven to be true.

**Example:** George Washington was the first president of the United States.

This statement is a fact. It can be proven to be true by researching the history of our country.

**Opinions** are statements that express how someone thinks or feels.

**Example:** George Washington was the greatest president the United States has ever had.

This statement is an opinion. Not everyone would agree that George Washington was the greatest president. Some people have the opinion that a different president was the greatest, such as Abraham Lincoln.

**Directions:** Read each sentence. Write **F** for fact or **O** for opinion.

_____     1.     There is three feet of snow on the ground.

_____     2.     A lot of snow makes the winter enjoyable.

_____     3.     Chris has a better swing set than Mary.

_____     4.     Both Chris and Mary have swing sets.

_____     5.     California is a state.

_____     6.     California is the best state in the west.

**Directions:** Write three facts and three opinions.

Facts:     1) _____

           2) _____

           3) _____

Opinions:  1) _____

           2) _____

           3) _____

16

# Get to the Point

The **main idea** is the most important idea, or main point, in a sentence, paragraph, or story.

**Directions:** Circle the main idea for each sentence.

1. Emily knew she would be late if she watched the end of the TV show.
   a. Emily likes watching TV.
   b. Emily is always running late.
   c. If Emily didn't leave, she would be late.

2. The dog was too strong and pulled Jason across the park with his leash.
   a. The dog is stronger than Jason.
   b. Jason is not very strong.
   c. Jason took the dog for a walk.

3. Jennifer took the book home so she could read it over and over.
   a. Jennifer loves to read.
   b. Jennifer loves the book.
   c. Jennifer is a good reader.

4. Jerome threw the baseball so hard it broke the window.
   a. Jerome throws baseballs very hard.
   b. Jerome was mad at the window.
   c. Jerome can't throw very straight.

5. Lori came home and decided to clean the kitchen for her parents.
   a. Lori is a very nice person.
   b. Lori did a favor for her parents.
   c. Lori likes to cook.

6. It was raining so hard that it was hard to see the road through the windshield.
   a. It always rains hard in April.
   b. The rain blurred our vision.
   c. It's hard to drive in the rain.

Name _____

# Winter Wonderland

The **main idea** of a story or report is a sentence that summarizes the most important point. If a story or report is only one paragraph in length, then the main idea is usually stated in the first sentence (topic sentence). If it is longer than one paragraph, then the main idea is a general sentence including all the important points of the story or report.

**Directions:** Read the story about snow fun. Then, draw an **X** in the blank for the main idea.

After a big snowfall, my friends and I enjoy playing in the snow. We bundle up in snow clothes at our homes, then meet with sleds at the hill by my house.

One by one, we take turns sledding down the hill to see who will go the farthest and the fastest. Sometimes we have a contest to see whose sled will reach the fence at the foot of the hill first.

When we tire of sledding, we may build a snowman or snowforts. Sometimes we have a friendly snowball fight.

The end of our snow fun comes too quickly, and we head home to warm houses, dry clothes, and hot chocolate.

1. What is the main idea?

   _____ Playing in the snow with friends is an enjoyable activity.

   _____ Sledding in the snow is fast and fun.

If you selected the first option, you are correct. The paragraphs discuss the enjoyable things friends do on a snowy day.

The second option is not correct because the entire story is not about sledding. Only the second paragraph discusses sledding. The other paragraphs discuss the additional ways friends have fun in the snow.

2. Write a paragraph about what you like to do on snowy days. Remember to make the first sentence your main idea.

   _____

   _____

# Ask It, State It

A **statement** tells some kind of information. It is followed by a period (.).

**Examples:** It is a rainy day. We are going to the beach next summer.

A **question** asks for a specific piece of information. It is followed by a question mark (?).

**Examples:** What is the weather like today? When are you going to the beach?

**Directions:** Write whether each sentence is a statement or question. The first one has been done for you.

1.  Jamie went for a walk at the zoo.　　　___statement___

2.  The leaves turn bright colors in the fall.　　_____

3.  When does the Easter Bunny arrive?　　_____

4.  Madeleine went to the new art school.　　_____

5.  Is school over at 3:30?　　_____

6.  Grandma and Grandpa are moving.　　_____

7.  Anthony went home.　　_____

8.  Did Malia go to Amy's house?　　_____

9.  Who went to work late?　　_____

10.  Ms. Gomez is a good teacher.　　_____

**Directions:** Write two statements and two questions below.

Statements: _____

_____

Questions: _____

_____

Name _____

# Taking Command

A **command** tells someone to do something. It is followed by a period (.).

**Examples:** Get your math book. Do your homework.

An **exclamation** shows strong feeling or excitement. It is followed by an exclamation mark (!).

**Examples:** Watch out for that car! Oh, no! There's a snake!

**Directions:** Write whether each sentence is a command or exclamation. The first one has been done for you.

1.  Please clean your room.                    _command_

2.  Wow! Those fireworks are beautiful!    _____

3.  Come to dinner now.                         _____

4.  Color the sky and water blue.            _____

5.  Trim the paper carefully.                   _____

6.  Hurry, here comes the bus!                _____

7.  Isn't that a lovely picture!                 _____

8.  Time to stop playing and clean up.      _____

9.  Brush your teeth before bedtime.        _____

10. Wash your hands before you eat!        _____

**Directions:** Write two commands and two exclamations below.

Commands: _____

_____

Exclamations: _____

_____

# Subject Matters

The **subject** of a sentence tells you who or what the sentence is about. A subject is either a common noun, a proper noun, or a pronoun.

**Examples:** Li went to the store. **Li** is the subject of the sentence.

The tired boys and girls walked home slowly.
**The tired boys and girls** is the subject of the sentence.

**Directions:** Underline the subject of each sentence. The first one has been done for you.

1. The <u>birthday cake</u> was pink and white.

2. Anthony celebrated his fourth birthday.

3. The tower of building blocks fell over.

4. On Saturday, our family will go to a movie.

5. The busy editor was writing sentences.

6. Seven children painted pictures.

7. Two happy dolphins played cheerfully on the surf.

8. A sand crab buried itself in the dunes.

**Directions:** Write a subject for each sentence.

1. <u>Chocolate-chip ice cream</u> was melting in the heat.

2. _____ ran down the steep hill.

3. _____ are full of colors.

4. _____ sang a cheerful tune.

5. _____ made her a beautiful dress.

6. _____ hopped, skipped, and jumped all the way home.

# Find the Action

The **predicate** of a sentence tells what the subject is doing. The predicate contains the action, linking, and/or helping verb.

**Examples:** Li went to the store.

**Went to the store** is the predicate.

The tired boys and girls walked home slowly.
**Walked home slowly** is the predicate.

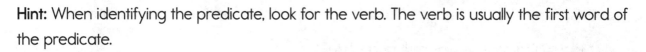

**Hint:** When identifying the predicate, look for the verb. The verb is usually the first word of the predicate.

**Directions:** Underline the predicate in each sentence with two lines. The first one has been done for you.

1. The choir sang joyfully.

2. Their song had both high and low notes.

3. Sal played the piano while they sang.

4. This Sunday the orchestra will have a concert in the park.

5. John is working hard on his homework.

6. He will write a report on electricity.

7. The report will tell about Ben Franklin's kite experiment.

8. Elena, Lily, and Amy played on the swings.

**Directions:** Write a predicate for each sentence.

1. Sam and Libby _____.

2. At school, the children _____.

3. The football team _____.

4. Seven silly serpents _____.

# Double Duty

A **compound subject** is a subject with two parts joined by the word **and** or another conjunction. Compound subjects share the same predicate.

**Example:**   Her shoes were covered with mud. Her ankles were covered with mud, too.

   **Compound subject:** Her shoes and ankles were covered with mud.

   The predicate in both sentences is **were covered with mud.**

**Directions:** Combine each pair of sentences into one sentence with a compound subject.

1.   Bill sneezed. Kassie sneezed.

   _____

2.   Carmen made cookies. Joey made cookies.

   _____

3.   Fruit flies are insects. Ladybugs are insects.

   _____

4.   The girls are planning a dance. The boys are planning a dance.

   _____

5.   Our dog ran after the ducks. Our cat ran after the ducks.

   _____

6.   Joshua got lost in the parking lot. DeShaun got lost in the parking lot.

   _____

Name _____

# It's Fine to Combine

A **compound predicate** is a predicate with two parts joined by the word **and** or another conjunction. Compound predicates share the same subject.

**Example:**  The baby grabbed the ball. The baby threw the ball.

**Compound predicate:** The baby grabbed the ball and threw it.

The subject in both sentences is **the baby**.

**Directions:** Combine each pair of sentences into one sentence to make a compound predicate.

1.  Leah jumped on her bike. Leah rode around the block.

    _____

2.  Father rolled out the pie crust. Father put the pie crust in the pan.

    _____

3.  Colin slipped on the snow. Colin nearly fell down.

    _____

4.  My friend lives in a green house. My friend rides a red bicycle.

    _____

5.  I opened the magazine. I began to read it quietly.

    _____

6.  My father bought a new plaid shirt. My father wore his new red tie.

    _____

    _____

# Nouns All Around

**Common nouns** name general people, places and things.

**Examples:** boy, girl, cat, dog, park, city, building

**Proper nouns** name specific people, places and things.

**Examples:** Owen, Mary, Fluffy, Rover, Central Park,
Chicago, Empire State Building

Proper nouns begin with capital letters.

**Directions:** Read the following nouns. On the blanks, indicate whether the nouns are common or proper. The first two have been done for you.

| | | | | | |
|---|---|---|---|---|---|
| 1. | New York City | proper | 7. | Dr. DiCarlo | _____ |
| 2. | house | common | 8. | man | _____ |
| 3. | car | _____ | 9. | Rock River | _____ |
| 4. | Ohio | _____ | 10. | building | _____ |
| 5. | river | _____ | 11. | lawyer | _____ |
| 6. | Rocky Mountains | _____ | 12. | Grand Canyon | _____ |

On another sheet of paper, write proper nouns for the above common nouns.

**Directions:** Read the following sentences. Underline the common nouns. Circle the proper nouns.

1. Addy's birthday is Friday, October 7.

2. She likes having her birthday in a fall month.

3. Her friends will meet her at the Video Arcade for a party.

4. Ms. McCarthy and Mr. Landry will help with the birthday party games.

5. Addy's friends will play video games all afternoon.

# Plural Power

Nouns come in two forms: singular and plural. When a noun is **singular**, it means there is only one person, place, or thing.

**Examples:** car, swing, box, truck, slide, bus

When a noun is **plural**, it means there is more than one person, place, or thing.

**Examples:** two cars, four trucks, three swings, five slides, six boxes, three buses

Usually an **s** is added to most nouns to make them plural. However, if the noun ends in **s, x, ch**, or **sh**, then **es** is added to make it plural.

**Directions:** Write the singular or plural form of each word.

| | Singular | Plural | | | Singular | Plural |
|---|---|---|---|---|---|---|
| 1. | car | _____ | 7. | _____ | tricks |
| 2. | bush | _____ | 8. | mess | _____ |
| 3. | wish | _____ | 9. | box | _____ |
| 4. | _____ | foxes | 10. | dish | _____ |
| 5. | _____ | rules | 11. | _____ | boats |
| 6. | stitch | _____ | 12. | path | _____ |

**Directions:** Rewrite the following sentences and change the bold nouns from singular to plural or from plural to singular. The first one has been done for you.

1. She took a **book** to school.

   <u>She took books to school.</u>

2. Tommy made **wishes** at his birthday party.

   _____

3. The **fox** ran away from the **hunters**.

   _____

4. The **houses** were painted white.

   _____

# Breaking the Rules

Some words in the English language do not follow any of the plural rules discussed earlier. These words may not change at all from singular to plural, or they may completely change spellings.

| No Change | Examples: | Complete Change | Examples: |
|---|---|---|---|
| **Singular** | **Plural** | **Singular** | **Plural** |
| deer | deer | goose | geese |
| pants | pants | ox | oxen |
| scissors | scissors | man | men |
| moose | moose | child | children |
| sheep | sheep | leaf | leaves |

**Directions:** Write the singular or plural form of each word. Use a dictionary to help if necessary.

| | Singular | Plural | | | Singular | Plural |
|---|---|---|---|---|---|---|
| 1. | moose | _____ | 6. | | leaf | _____ |
| 2. | woman | _____ | 7. | | _____ | sheep |
| 3. | _____ | deer | 8. | | scissors | _____ |
| 4. | _____ | children | 9. | | tooth | _____ |
| 5. | _____ | hooves | 10. | | wharf | _____ |

**Directions:** Write four sentences of your own using two singular and two plural words from above.

_____

_____

_____

_____

# Pronoun Lowdown

A **pronoun** is a word that takes the place of a noun in a sentence.

**Examples:** I, my, mine, me

we, our, ours, us

you, your, yours

he, his, him

she, her, hers

it, its

they, their, theirs, them

**Directions:** Underline the pronouns in each sentence.

1. Bring them to us as soon as you are finished.

2. She has been my best friend for many years.

3. They should be here soon.

4. We enjoyed our trip to the Mustard Museum.

5. Would you be able to help us with the project on Saturday?

6. Our homeroom teacher will not be here tomorrow.

7. My uncle said that he will be leaving soon for Australia.

8. Hurry! Could you please open the door for him?

# Verb Alert

**Verbs** show action or state of being. There are three kinds of verbs: action verbs, linking verbs, and helping verbs.

An **action verb** tells the action of a sentence.

**Examples:** run, hop, skip, sleep, jump, talk, snore
Michael **ran** to the store. **Ran** is the action verb.

A **linking verb** joins the subject and predicate of a sentence.

**Examples:** am, is, are, was, were
Michael **was** at the store. **Was** is the linking verb.

A **helping verb** is used with an action or linking verb to "help" express the subject's action or state of being.

**Examples:** am, is, are, was, were
Matthew **was** helping Michael. **Was** helps the action verb **helping**.

**Directions:** Read the following sentences. Underline the verbs. Above each, write **A** for action verb, **L** for linking verb, or **H** for helping verb. The first one has been done for you.

1. Amy _jumps_ rope.  *(A)*

2. Kahlil was jumping rope, too.

3. They were working on their homework.

4. The math problem requires a lot of thinking.

5. Addition problems are fun to do.

6. The baby sleeps in the afternoon.

7. Grandma is napping also.

8. Sam is going to bed.

9. Jackson paints a lovely picture of the sea.

10. The colors in the picture are soft and pale.

# Tense Tips

Not only do verbs usually tell the action of a sentence but they also tell when the action takes place. This is called the **verb tense**. There are three verb tenses: past, present, and future tense.

**Present-tense verbs** tell what is happening now.

**Example:**   Jane **spells** words with long vowel sounds.

**Past-tense verbs** tell about action that has already happened. Past-tense verbs are usually formed by adding **ed** to the verb.

**Example:**   stay — stayed
              Vidas **stayed** home yesterday.

Past-tense verbs can also be made by adding helping verbs **was** or **were** before the verb and adding **ing** to the verb.

**Example:**   talk — was talking
              Sally **was talking** to her mom.

**Future-tense verbs** tell what will happen in the future. Future-tense verbs are made by putting the word **will** before the verb.

**Example:**   paint — will paint
              Amelia and Ana-Maria **will paint** the house.

**Directions:** Read the following verbs. Write whether the verb tense is past, present or future.

| | Verb | Tense | | | Verb | Tense |
|---|---|---|---|---|---|---|
| 1. | watches | present | 8. | writes | |
| 2. | wanted | _____ | 9. | vaulted | _____ |
| 3. | will eat | _____ | 10. | were sleeping | _____ |
| 4. | was squawking | _____ | 11. | will sing | _____ |
| 5. | yawns | _____ | 12. | is speaking | _____ |
| 6. | crawled | _____ | 13. | will cook | _____ |
| 7. | will hunt | _____ | 14. | likes | _____ |

# That's History!

**Irregular verbs** change completely in the past tense. Unlike regular verbs, past-tense forms of irregular verbs are not formed by adding **ed**.

**Example:** The past tense of **go** is **went**.

Other verbs change some letters to form the past tense.

**Example:** The past tense of **break** is **broke**.

A **helping verb** helps to tell about the past. **Has, have**, and **had** are helping verbs used with action verbs to show the action occurred in the past. The past-tense form of the irregular verb sometimes changes when a helping verb is added.

| Present Tense Irregular Verb | Past Tense Irregular Verb | Past Tense Irregular Verb With Helper |
|---|---|---|
| go | went | have/has/had gone |
| see | saw | have/has/had seen |
| do | did | have/has/had done |
| bring | brought | have/has/had brought |
| sing | sang | have/has/had sung |
| drive | drove | have/has/had driven |
| swim | swam | have/has/had swum |
| sleep | slept | have/has/had slept |

**Directions:** Choose four words from the chart. Write one sentence using the past-tense form of the verb without a helping verb. Write another sentence using the past-tense form with a helping verb.

1. _____

   _____

2. _____

   _____

3. _____

   _____

4. _____

   _____

# Prescription for Description

Adjectives tell more about nouns. Adjectives are describing words.

**Examples:** **scary** animals      **bright** glow      **wet** frog

**Directions:** Add at least two adjectives to each sentence below. Use your own words or words from the box.

| | | | | | | |
|---|---|---|---|---|---|---|
| pale | soft | sticky | burning | furry | glistening | peaceful |
| faint | shivering | slippery | gleaming | gentle | foggy | tangled |

**Example:**   The stripe was blue.

The wide stripe was light blue.

1. The frog had eyes.

_____

2. The house was a sight.

_____

3. A boy heard a noise.

_____

4. The girl tripped over a toad.

_____

5. A tiger ran through the room.

_____

6. They saw a glow in the window.

_____

# Absolutely Adverbs

Like adjectives, **adverbs** are describing words. They usually describe verbs. Adverbs tell how, when, or where action takes place.

| Examples: | How | When | Where |
|-----------|-----|------|-------|
| | slowly | yesterday | here |
| | gracefully | today | there |
| | swiftly | tomorrow | everywhere |
| | quickly | soon | |

How?
When?
Where?

**Hint:** To identify an adverb, locate the verb, then ask yourself if there are any words that tell how, when or where action takes place.

**Directions:** Read the following sentences. Underline the adverbs, then write whether they tell how, when or where. The first one has been done for you.

1. At the end of the day, the children ran <u>quickly</u> home from school.              how

2. They will have a spelling test tomorrow.              _____

3. Slowly, the children filed to their seats.              _____

4. The teacher sat here at her desk.              _____

5. She will pass the tests back later.              _____

6. The students received their grades happily.              _____

**Directions:** Write four sentences of your own using any of the adverbs above.

_____

_____

_____

_____

Name _____

# Join the Fun

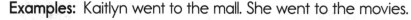

**Conjunctions** are joining words that can be used to combine sentences. Words such as **and, but, or, when,** and **after** are conjunctions.

**Examples:**  Kaitlyn went to the mall. She went to the movies.
Kaitlyn went to the mall, and she went to the movies.

We can have our vacation at home. We can vacation at the beach.
We can have our vacation at home, or we can vacation at the beach.

Jada fell on the playground. She did not hurt herself.
Jada fell on the playground, but she did not hurt herself.

**Note:** The conjunctions **after** or **when** are usually placed at the beginning of the sentence.

**Example:**  Amrita went to the store. She went to the gas station.
After Amrita went to the store, she went to the gas station.

**Directions:** Combine the following sentences using a conjunction.

1. Peter fell down the steps. He broke his foot. (and)

   _____

2. I visited New York. I would like to see Chicago. (but)

   _____

3. Rosie can edit books. She can write stories. (or)

   _____

4. He played in the barn. John started to sneeze. (when)

   _____

5. The team won the playoffs. They went to the championships. (after)

   _____

**Directions:** Write three sentences of your own using the conjunctions **and, but, or, when** and **after.**

_____

_____

_____

# Common Commas

Use a comma to separate the number of the day of a month and the year. Do not use a comma to separate the month and year if no day is given.

**Examples:** June 14, 2010

June 2009

Use a comma after **yes** or **no** when it is the first word in a sentence.

**Examples:** Yes, I will do it right now.

No, I don't want any.

**Directions:** Write **C** if the sentence is punctuated correctly. Draw an **X** if the sentence is not punctuated correctly. The first one has been done for you.

**C**   1.   No, I don't plan to attend.

_____   2.   I told them, oh yes, I would go.

_____   3.   Her birthday is March 13, 1995.

_____   4.   He was born in May, 2008.

_____   5.   Yes, of course I like you!

_____   6.   No I will not be there.

_____   7.   They left for vacation on February, 14.

_____   8.   No, today is Monday.

_____   9.   The program was first shown on August 12, 1991.

_____   10.   In September, 2030 how old will you be?

_____   11.   He turned 12 years old on November, 13.

_____   12.   I said no, I will not come no matter what!

# The Comma Connection

Use a comma to separate words in a series. A comma is used after each word in a series but is not needed before the last word. Both ways are correct. In your own writing, be consistent about which style you use.

**Examples:**   We ate apples, oranges, and pears.

           We ate apples, oranges and pears.

Always use a comma between the name of a city and a state.

**Examples:**   She lives in Fresno, California.

           He lives in Wilmington, Delaware.

**Directions:** Write **C** if the sentence is punctuated correctly. Draw an **X** if the sentence is not punctuated correctly. The first one has been done for you.

__X__   1.   She ordered shoes, dresses and shirts to be sent to her home in Oakland California.

_____   2.   No one knew her pets' names were Fido, Spot and Tiger.

_____   3.   He likes green beans lima beans, and corn on the cob.

_____   4.   Notebooks, pens and pencils are all needed for school.

_____   5.   Send your letters to her in College Park, Maryland.

_____   6.   Orlando Florida is the home of Disney World.

_____   7.   Mickey, Minnie, Goofy and Daisy are all favorites of mine.

_____   8.   Send your letter to her in Reno, Nevada.

_____   9.   Before he lived in New York, City he lived in San Diego, California.

_____   10.   She mailed postcards, and letters to him in Lexington, Kentucky.

_____   11.   Teacups, saucers, napkins, and silverware were piled high.

# Good Reads

All words in the title of a book are underlined. Underlined words go in italics when typed.

**Examples:** The Hunt for Red October was a best-seller!
(*The Hunt for Red October*)

Have you read Lost in Space?
(*Lost in Space*)

**Directions:** Underline the book titles in these sentences. The first one has been done for you.

1.   The Dinosaur Poster Book is for eight-year-olds.

2.   Have you read Lion Dancer by Kate Waters?

3.   Baby Dinosaurs and Giant Dinosaurs were both written by Peter Dodson.

4.   Have you heard of the book That's What Friends Are For by Carol Adorjan?

5.   J.B. Stamper wrote a book called The Totally Terrific Valentine Party Book.

6.   The teacher read Almost Ten and a Half aloud to our class.

7.   Marrying Off Mom is about a girl who tries to get her widowed mother to start dating.

8.   The Snow and The Fire are the second and third books by author Caroline Cooney.

9.   The title sounds silly, but Goofbang Value Daze really is the name of a book!

10.   A book about space exploration is The Day We Walked on the Moon by George Sullivan.

11.   Alice and the Birthday Giant tells about a giant who came to a girl's birthday party.

# You Said It!

Use quotation marks (" ") before and after the exact words of a speaker.

**Examples:** I asked Aunt Martha, "How do you feel?"

"I feel awful," Aunt Martha replied.

Do not put quotation marks around words that report what the speaker said.

**Examples:** Aunt Martha said she felt awful.

I asked Aunt Martha how she felt.

**Directions:** Write **C** if the sentence is punctuated correctly. Draw an **X** if the sentence is not punctuated correctly. The first one has been done for you.

**C** 1. "I want it right now!" she demanded angrily.

_____ 2. "Do you want it now? I asked."

_____ 3. She said "she felt better" now.

_____ 4. Her exact words were, "I feel much better now!"

_____ 5. "I am so thrilled to be here!" he shouted.

_____ 6. "Yes, I will attend," she replied.

_____ 7. Elizabeth said "she was unhappy."

_____ 8. "I'm unhappy," Elizabeth reported.

_____ 9. "Did you know her mother?" I asked.

_____ 10. I asked "whether you knew her mother."

_____ 11. I wondered, "What will dessert be?"

_____ 12. "Which will it be, salt or pepper?" the waiter asked.

# On the Run

A **run-on sentence** occurs when two or more sentences are joined together without punctuation.

**Examples:** **Run-on sentence:** I lost my way once did you?

**Two sentences with correct punctuation:** I lost my way once. Did you?

**Run-on sentence:** I found the recipe it was not hard to follow.

**Two sentences with correct punctuation:** I found the recipe. It was not hard to follow.

**Directions:** Rewrite the run-on sentences correctly with periods, exclamation points, and question marks. The first one has been done for you.

1. Did you take my umbrella I can't find it anywhere!

   _Did you take my umbrella? I can't find it anywhere!_

2. How can you stand that noise I can't!

   _____

3. The cookies are gone I see only crumbs.

   _____

4. The dogs were barking they were hungry.

   _____

5. She is quite ill please call a doctor immediately!

   _____

6. The clouds came up we knew the storm would hit soon.

   _____

7. You weren't home he stopped by this morning.

   _____

# Putting It Together

**Directions:** Make each pair of sentences into one sentence. (You may have to change the verbs for some sentences—from **is** to **are**, for example.)

**Example:**  Our house was flooded. Our car was flooded.

### Our house and car were flooded.

1. Dmitry sees a glow.                    Carrie sees a glow.

   _____

2. Our new stove came today.              Our new refrigerator came today.

   _____

3. The pond is full of toads.             The field is full of toads.

   _____

4. Stripes are on the flag.               Stars are on the flag.

   _____

5. The ducks took flight.                 The geese took flight.

   _____

6. Joe reads stories.                     Dana reads stories.

   _____

# Busy Kids

**Directions:** Read about settler children. Then, complete the list of main points at the end of the article.

In the 1700s and 1800s, many children from other countries came with their parents to America. In the beginning, they had no time to go to school. They had to help their families work in the fields, care for the animals, and clean the house. They also helped care for their younger brothers and sisters.

Sometimes settler children helped build houses and schools. Usually, these early school buildings were just one room. There was only one teacher for all the children. Settler children were very happy when they could attend school.

Because settler children worked so much, they had little time to play. There were not many things settler children could do just for fun. One pastime was gardening. Weeding their gardens taught them how to be orderly. Children sometimes made gifts out of the things they grew.

The settlers also encouraged their children to sing. Each one was expected to play at least one musical instrument. Parents wanted their children to walk, ride horses, visit friends and relatives, and read nonfiction books.

Most settler children did not have many toys. The toys they owned were made by their parents and grandparents. They were usually made of cloth or carved from wood. The children made up games with string, like "cat's cradle." They also made things out of wood, such as seesaws. Settler children did not have all the toys we have today, but they managed to have fun anyway!

The main points of this article are:

1. Settler children worked hard.

2. Settler children had many jobs.

3. _____

4. _____

5. _____

**Directions:** When you summarize, you are writing a shorter article that contains only the main points. Use the main points to write a summary of this article on a separate sheet of paper.

# Finding Your Place

Place value is the value of a digit, or numeral, shown by the digit's location in the number. For example, in 1,234, 1 has the place value of thousands, 2 is hundreds, 3 is tens, and 4 is ones.

**Directions:** Write the numbers in the correct boxes to find how far the car has traveled.

one thousand

six hundreds

eight ones

nine ten thousands

four tens

two millions

five hundred thousands

| millions | hundred thousands | ten thousands | thousands | hundreds | tens | ones |
|---|---|---|---|---|---|---|
| | | | | | | |

How many miles has the car traveled? _____

**Directions:** In the number . . .

2,386 _____ is in the ones place.

4,957 _____ is in the hundreds place.

102,432 _____ is in the ten thousands place.

1,743,998 _____ is in the millions place.

9,301,671 _____ is in the hundred thousands place.

# Adding On

When adding two-, three-, and four-digit numbers, add the ones first, then tens, hundreds, thousands, and so on.

**Example:**

| Tens | Ones |
|------|------|
| 5 | 4 |
| + 2 | 5 |
| | 9 |

| Tens | Ones |
|------|------|
| 5 | 4 |
| + 2 | 5 |
| 7 | 9 |

**Directions:** Add the following numbers.

```
   81          67          34         730
 + 23        + 22        + 82       + 265
```

```
   76       1,803         523         267
 + 73      + 1,104       + 476       +  12
```

```
                        4,254         111
                       +  545       +  82
```

```
                          164         727
                       +  425       +  51
```

Name _____

# Regrouping Roundup

**Directions:** Subtract using regrouping.

Examples:

$$\begin{array}{r} 23 \\ -18 \\ \hline \end{array} \qquad \begin{array}{r} {}^{1}2\!\!\!/3 \\ -18 \\ \hline 5 \end{array} \qquad \begin{array}{r} 243 \\ -96 \\ \hline \end{array} \qquad \begin{array}{r} {}^{1\;13}2\!\!\!/4\!\!\!/3 \\ -96 \\ \hline 147 \end{array}$$

$$\begin{array}{r} 81 \\ -53 \\ \hline \end{array} \qquad \begin{array}{r} 76 \\ -49 \\ \hline \end{array} \qquad \begin{array}{r} 94 \\ -38 \\ \hline \end{array} \qquad \begin{array}{r} 156 \\ -77 \\ \hline \end{array} \qquad \begin{array}{r} 341 \\ -83 \\ \hline \end{array}$$

$$\begin{array}{r} 568 \\ -173 \\ \hline \end{array} \qquad \begin{array}{r} 806 \\ -738 \\ \hline \end{array} \qquad \begin{array}{r} 743 \\ -550 \\ \hline \end{array} \qquad \begin{array}{r} 903 \\ -336 \\ \hline \end{array} \qquad \begin{array}{r} 647 \\ -289 \\ \hline \end{array}$$

$$\begin{array}{r} 730 \\ -518 \\ \hline \end{array} \qquad \begin{array}{r} 961 \\ -846 \\ \hline \end{array} \qquad \begin{array}{r} 573 \\ -76 \\ \hline \end{array} \qquad \begin{array}{r} 604 \\ -55 \\ \hline \end{array} \qquad \begin{array}{r} 265 \\ -19 \\ \hline \end{array}$$

$$\begin{array}{r} 111 \\ -82 \\ \hline \end{array} \qquad \begin{array}{r} 358 \\ -99 \\ \hline \end{array} \qquad \begin{array}{r} 147 \\ -49 \\ \hline \end{array}$$

$$\begin{array}{r} 180 \\ -106 \\ \hline \end{array} \qquad \begin{array}{r} 325 \\ -68 \\ \hline \end{array} \qquad \begin{array}{r} 873 \\ -35 \\ \hline \end{array}$$

# Round Up, Round Down

When rounding to the nearest hundred, the key number is in the tens place. If the tens digit is 5 or larger, round up to the nearest hundred. If the tens digit is 4 or less, round down to the nearest hundred.

**Examples:**

Round 871 to the nearest hundred.

7 is the key digit.

If it is more than 5, round up.

Answer: <u>900</u>

Round 421 to the nearest hundred.

2 is the key digit.

If it is less than 4, round down.

Answer: <u>400</u>

**Directions:** Round these numbers to the nearest hundred.

255 _____      368 _____      443 _____

562 _____      698 _____      99 _____

812 _____      592 _____      124 _____

When rounding to the nearest thousand, the key number is in the hundreds place. If the hundreds digit is 5 or larger, round up to the nearest thousand. If the hundreds digit is 4 or less, round down to the nearest thousand.

**Examples:**

Round 7,932 to the nearest thousand.

9 is the key digit.

If it is more than 5, round up.

Answer: <u>8,000</u>

Round 1,368 to the nearest thousand.

3 is the key digit.

If it is less than 4, round down.

Answer: <u>1,000</u>

**Directions:** Round these numbers to the nearest thousand.

8,631 _____      1,248 _____      798 _____

999 _____      6,229 _____      8,461 _____

9,654 _____      4,963 _____      99,923 _____

# Can't Wait to Estimate!

Estimating is used for certain mathematical calculations. For example, to figure the cost of several items, round their prices to the nearest dollar, then add up the approximate cost. A store clerk, on the other hand, needs to know the exact prices in order to charge the correct amount. To estimate to the nearest hundred, round up numbers over 50. **Example:** 251 is rounded up to 300. Round down numbers less than 50. **Example:** 128 is rounded down to 100.

**Directions:** In the following situations, write whether an exact or estimated answer should be used.

**Example:** You make a deposit in your bank account. Do you want an estimated total or an exact total?          <u>Exact</u>

1.  Your family just ate dinner at a restaurant. Your parents are trying to calculate the tip for your server. Should they estimate by rounding or use exact numbers?          _____

2.  You are at the store buying candy, and you want to know if you have enough money to pay for it. Should you estimate or use exact numbers?          _____

3.  Some friends are planning a trip from New York City to Washington, D.C. They need to know about how far they will travel in miles. Should they estimate or use exact numbers?          _____

4.  You plan a trip to the zoo. Beforehand, you call the zoo for the price of admission. Should the person at the zoo tell you an estimated or exact price?          _____

5.  The teacher is grading your papers. Should your scores be exact or estimated?          _____

# Don't Count Your Eggs—Multiply!

Follow the steps for multiplying a one-digit number by a two-digit number using regrouping.

**Example: Step 1:** Multiply the ones.
Regroup.

```
  2
 54
x 7
  8
```

**Step 2:** Multiply the tens.
Add two tens.

```
  2
 54
x 7
378
```

**Directions:** Multiply.

```
  27        63        52        91        45
x  3      x  4      x  5      x  9      x  7
```

```
  64        76        93        87        66
x  5      x  3      x  6      x  4      x  7
```

```
  47        64        51
x  8      x  9      x  8
```

The chickens on the Boudreaux farm produce 48 dozen eggs each day. How many dozen eggs do they produce in 7 days? _____

Name _____

# Dairy Delights

Follow the steps for multiplying a two-digit number by a two-digit number using regrouping.

**Example:** Step 1:  Multiply the ones.
Regroup.

Step 2:  Multiply the tens.
Regroup. Add.

$$
\begin{array}{r} 63 \\ \times\ 68 \\ \end{array}
\qquad
\begin{array}{r} {\scriptstyle 2} \\ 63 \\ \times\ 68 \\ \hline 504 \\ \end{array}
\qquad
\begin{array}{r} {\scriptstyle 1} \\ 63 \\ \times\ 68 \\ \hline 3{,}780 \\ \end{array}
\qquad
\begin{array}{r} 63 \\ \times\ 68 \\ \hline 504 \\ +\ 3{,}780 \\ \hline 4{,}284 \\ \end{array}
$$

**Directions:** Multiply.

$$
\begin{array}{r} 12 \\ \times\ 55 \\ \hline \end{array}
\qquad
\begin{array}{r} 27 \\ \times\ 15 \\ \hline \end{array}
\qquad
\begin{array}{r} 65 \\ \times\ 27 \\ \hline \end{array}
\qquad
\begin{array}{r} 19 \\ \times\ 39 \\ \hline \end{array}
\qquad
\begin{array}{r} 99 \\ \times\ 13 \\ \hline \end{array}
$$

$$
\begin{array}{r} 43 \\ \times\ 26 \\ \hline \end{array}
\qquad
\begin{array}{r} 38 \\ \times\ 17 \\ \hline \end{array}
\qquad
\begin{array}{r} 53 \\ \times\ 86 \\ \hline \end{array}
\qquad
\begin{array}{r} 47 \\ \times\ 72 \\ \hline \end{array}
\qquad
\begin{array}{r} 57 \\ \times\ 62 \\ \hline \end{array}
$$

$$
\begin{array}{r} 27 \\ \times\ 54 \\ \hline \end{array}
\qquad
\begin{array}{r} 93 \\ \times\ 45 \\ \hline \end{array}
\qquad
\begin{array}{r} 64 \\ \times\ 16 \\ \hline \end{array}
\qquad
\begin{array}{r} 53 \\ \times\ 23 \\ \hline \end{array}
$$

The Polanski farm has 24 cows that each produce 52 quarts of milk a day. How many quarts are produced each day altogether? _____

# At the Pumpkin Patch

**Directions:** Multiply. Regroup when needed.

**Example:**

$$
\begin{array}{r}
563 \\
\times\ 248 \\
\hline
4{,}504 \\
22{,}520 \\
+\ 112{,}600 \\
\hline
139{,}624
\end{array}
$$

**Hint:** When Multiplying by the tens, start writing the number in the tens place. When multiplying by the hundreds, start in the hundreds place.

$$
\begin{array}{r}
842 \\
\times\ 167 \\
\hline
\end{array}
\qquad
\begin{array}{r}
932 \\
\times\ 272 \\
\hline
\end{array}
\qquad
\begin{array}{r}
759 \\
\times\ 468 \\
\hline
\end{array}
\qquad
\begin{array}{r}
531 \\
\times\ 556 \\
\hline
\end{array}
$$

$$
\begin{array}{r}
383 \\
\times\ 476 \\
\hline
\end{array}
\qquad
\begin{array}{r}
523 \\
\times\ 349 \\
\hline
\end{array}
\qquad
\begin{array}{r}
229 \\
\times\ 189 \\
\hline
\end{array}
\qquad
\begin{array}{r}
738 \\
\times\ 513 \\
\hline
\end{array}
$$

James grows pumpkins on his farm. He has 362 rows of pumpkins. There are 593 pumpkins in each row. How many pumpkins does James grow?  _____

Name _____

# Leftovers

Sometimes groups of objects or numbers cannot be divided into equal groups. The **remainder** is the number left over in the quotient of a division problem. The remainder must be smaller than the divisor.

**Example:** Divide 18 butterflies into groups of 5.
You have 3 equal groups,
with 3 butterflies left over.     $18 \div 5 = 3$ R3

or

$$\begin{array}{r} 3\,\text{R}3 \\ 5\overline{)18} \\ -15 \\ \hline 3 \end{array}$$

**Directions:** Divide. Some problems may have remainders.

$9\overline{)84}$     $7\overline{)65}$     $8\overline{)25}$     $5\overline{)35}$     $5\overline{)34}$

$4\overline{)25}$     $6\overline{)56}$     $4\overline{)7}$     $4\overline{)16}$     $8\overline{)37}$

$7\overline{)27}$     $2\overline{)5}$     $2\overline{)4}$     $8\overline{)73}$     $4\overline{)9}$

$9\overline{)46}$     $5\overline{)17}$     $2\overline{)3}$     $4\overline{)13}$     $5\overline{)25}$

# Check It Out!

To check a division problem, multiply the quotient by the divisor. Add the remainder. The answer will be the dividend.

**Example:**

```
          quotient
              58 R1
divisor →  3) 175
              - 15
   dividend   25
              - 24
remainder ──→  1
```

```
 58  ← quotient
x 3  ← divisor
174
+ 1  ← remainder
175  ← dividend
```

**Directions:** Divide each problem, then draw a line from the division problem to the correct checking problem.

| 33 | 53 | 97 | 135 | 113 | 119 |
|---|---|---|---|---|---|
| x 7 | x 7 | x 7 | x 7 | x 7 | x 7 |
|  | + 2 | + 3 | + 1 | + 1 | + 1 |

```
   97 R3
7) 682
 - 63
   52
 - 49
    3
```

7) 231    7) 373    7) 792    7) 834    7) 946

The toy factory puts 7 robot dogs in each box. The factory has 256 robot dogs. How many boxes will they need?

_____

# The Drive to Divide

**Directions:** Divide. Then, check each answer on another sheet of paper by multiplying it by the divisor and adding the remainder.

**Example:**

$$\begin{array}{r} 2 \\ 12\overline{)256} \\ -24 \\ \hline 1 \end{array}$$

$$\begin{array}{r} 21 \text{ R}4 \\ 12\overline{)256} \\ -24 \\ \hline 16 \\ -12 \\ \hline 4 \end{array}$$

**Check:**

$$\begin{array}{r} 21 \\ \times 12 \\ \hline 42 \\ +210 \\ \hline 252 \\ +\ \ 4 \\ \hline 256 \end{array}$$

$27\overline{)880}$     $81\overline{)913}$     $65\overline{)790}$     $42\overline{)674}$     $67\overline{)823}$

$72\overline{)977}$     $54\overline{)743}$     $45\overline{)863}$     $24\overline{)432}$     $18\overline{)372}$

$28\overline{)175}$     $49\overline{)538}$     $77\overline{)936}$     $37\overline{)603}$     $63\overline{)835}$

The Allen farm has 882 chickens. The chickens are kept in 21 coops. How many chickens are there in each coop? _____

# Batter Up!

An **average** is found by adding two or more quantities and dividing by the number of quantities.

**Example:**   **Step 1:** Find the sum of the numbers.

   $24 + 36 + 30 = 90$

   **Step 2:** Divide by the number of quantities.

   $90 ÷ 3 = 30$

   The average is 30.

**Directions:** Find the average of each group of numbers. Draw a line from each problem to the correct average.

| | |
|---|---|
| $12 + 14 + 29 + 1 =$ | 410 |
| $4 + 10 + 25 =$ | 83 |
| $33 + 17 + 14 + 20 + 16 =$ | 40 |
| $782 + 276 + 172 =$ | 15 |
| $81 + 82 + 91 + 78 =$ | 13 |
| $21 + 34 + 44 =$ | 33 |
| $14 + 24 + 10 + 31 + 5 + 6 =$ | 14 |
| $278 + 246 =$ | 20 |
| $48 + 32 + 18 + 62 =$ | 262 |

A baseball player had 3 hits in game one, 2 hits in game two and 4 hits in game three. How many hits did she average over the three games?   _____

# Flower Power

When adding fractions with the same denominator, the denominator stays the same. Add only the numerators.

**Example:**   numerator $\frac{1}{8}$ + $\frac{2}{8}$ = $\frac{3}{8}$
denominator

**Directions:** Add the fractions on the flowers. Begin in the center of each flower and add each petal. The first one is done for you.

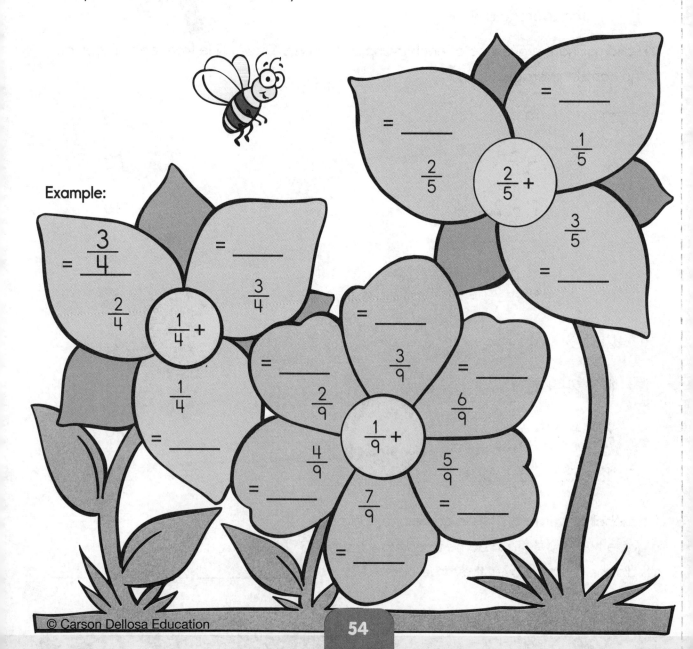

Name _____

# Fraction Subtraction

When subtracting fractions with the same denominator, the denominator stays the same. Subtract only the numerators.

**Directions:** Solve the problems, working from left to right. As you find each answer, copy the letter from the key into the numbered blanks. The answer is the name of a famous American. The first one is done for you.

| | | | | | | |
|---|---|---|---|---|---|---|
| T $\frac{1}{8}$ | F $\frac{4}{12}$ | E $\frac{3}{9}$ | R $\frac{7}{16}$ | Q $\frac{1}{32}$ | A $\frac{1}{12}$ | N $\frac{2}{6}$ |
| P $\frac{5}{24}$ | E $\frac{2}{7}$ | O $\frac{2}{9}$ | O $\frac{2}{8}$ | M $\frac{1}{3}$ | R $\frac{12}{15}$ | O $\frac{11}{15}$ |
| H $\frac{1}{4}$ | J $\frac{3}{12}$ | F $\frac{4}{8}$ | Y $\frac{8}{20}$ | S $\frac{5}{20}$ | S $\frac{3}{5}$ | |

1. $\frac{3}{8} - \frac{2}{8} = \frac{1}{8}$

2. $\frac{2}{4} - \frac{1}{4} = $ _____

3. $\frac{5}{9} - \frac{3}{9} = $ _____

4. $\frac{2}{3} - \frac{1}{3} = $ _____

5. $\frac{8}{12} - \frac{7}{12} = $ _____

6. $\frac{4}{5} - \frac{1}{5} = $ _____

7. $\frac{6}{12} - \frac{3}{12} = $ _____

8. $\frac{4}{9} - \frac{1}{9} = $ _____

9. $\frac{11}{12} - \frac{7}{12} = $ _____

10. $\frac{7}{8} - \frac{3}{8} = $ _____

11. $\frac{4}{7} - \frac{2}{7} = $ _____

12. $\frac{14}{16} - \frac{7}{16} = $ _____

13. $\frac{18}{20} - \frac{13}{20} = $ _____

14. $\frac{13}{15} - \frac{2}{15} = $ _____

15. $\frac{5}{6} - \frac{3}{6} = $ _____

Who helped write the Declaration of Independence?

T __ __ __ __ __   __ __ __ __ __ __ __ __ __
1  2  3  4  5  6   7  8  9 10 11 12 13 14 15

# Any Way You Slice It

Equivalent fractions are two different fractions that represent the same number.

**Example:**  $\dfrac{1}{2}$ = $\dfrac{3}{6}$

**Directions:** Complete these equivalent fractions.

$\dfrac{1}{3} = \dfrac{}{6}$ $\qquad\qquad$ $\dfrac{1}{2} = \dfrac{}{4}$ $\qquad\qquad$ $\dfrac{3}{4} = \dfrac{}{8}$ $\qquad\qquad$ $\dfrac{1}{3} = \dfrac{}{9}$

**Directions:** Circle the figures that show a fraction equivalent to figure a. Write the fraction for the shaded area under each figure.

a.

b.

c.

d.

_____   _____   _____   _____

e.

f.

g.

h.

_____   _____   _____   _____

To find an equivalent fraction, multiply both parts of the fraction by the same number.

**Example:** $\dfrac{2}{3} \times \dfrac{3}{3} = \dfrac{6}{9}$

**Directions:** Find an equivalent fraction.

$\dfrac{1}{4} = \dfrac{}{8}$ $\qquad\qquad$ $\dfrac{3}{4} = \dfrac{}{16}$ $\qquad\qquad$ $\dfrac{4}{5} = \dfrac{8}{}$ $\qquad\qquad$ $\dfrac{3}{8} = \dfrac{}{24}$

# Finding Home

Reducing a fraction means to find the greatest common factor and divide.

**Example:** $\dfrac{5}{15}$  factors of 5: 1, 5

factors of 15: 1, 3, 5, 15

5 is the greatest common factor.
Divide both the numerator and
denominator by 5.

$5 \div 5 = \dfrac{1}{3}$
$15 \div 5 =$

**Directions:** Reduce each fraction. Circle the correct answer.

$\dfrac{2}{4} = \dfrac{1}{2}, \dfrac{1}{6}, \dfrac{1}{8}$

$\dfrac{3}{9} = \dfrac{1}{6}, \dfrac{1}{3}, \dfrac{3}{6}$

$\dfrac{5}{10} = \dfrac{1}{5}, \dfrac{1}{2}, \dfrac{5}{6}$

$\dfrac{4}{12} = \dfrac{1}{4}, \dfrac{1}{3}, \dfrac{2}{3}$

$\dfrac{10}{15} = \dfrac{2}{3}, \dfrac{2}{5}, \dfrac{2}{7}$

$\dfrac{12}{14} = \dfrac{1}{8}, \dfrac{6}{7}, \dfrac{3}{5}$

**Directions:** Find the way home. Color the boxes with fractions equivalent to $\frac{1}{8}$ and $\frac{1}{3}$.

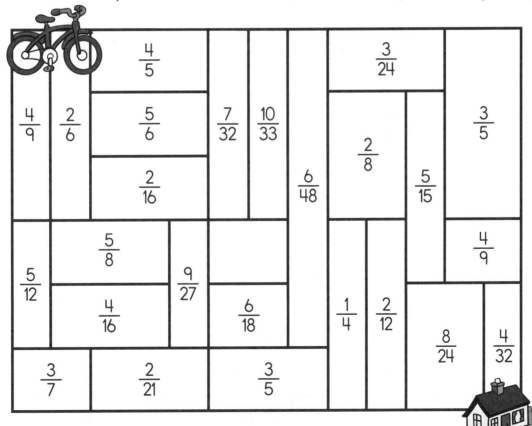

# Mix It up!

A mixed number is a number written as a whole number and a fraction, such as $6\frac{5}{8}$.

To change a fraction into a mixed number, divide the denominator (bottom number) into the numerator (top number). Write the remainder over the denominator.

**Example:** $\frac{14}{6} = 2\frac{2}{6}$

$$6\overline{)14} \quad \begin{array}{r} 2\text{ R2} \\ \hline 14 \\ -12 \\ \hline 2 \end{array}$$

**Example:** $3\frac{1}{7} = \frac{22}{7}$ $\quad (7 \times 3) + 1 = \frac{22}{7}$

To change a mixed number into a fraction, multiply the denominator by the whole number, add the numerator and write it on top of the denominator.

**Directions:** Write each fraction as a mixed number. Write each mixed number as a fraction.

$\frac{21}{6} =$ _____ $\qquad \frac{24}{5} =$ _____ $\qquad \frac{10}{3} =$ _____ $\qquad \frac{21}{4} =$ _____

$\frac{11}{6} =$ _____ $\qquad \frac{13}{4} =$ _____ $\qquad \frac{12}{5} =$ _____ $\qquad \frac{10}{9} =$ _____

$4\frac{3}{8} = \frac{}{8}$ $\qquad 2\frac{1}{3} = \frac{}{3}$ $\qquad 4\frac{3}{5} = \frac{}{5}$ $\qquad 3\frac{4}{6} = \frac{}{6}$

$7\frac{1}{4} = \frac{}{4}$ $\qquad 2\frac{3}{5} = \frac{}{5}$ $\qquad 7\frac{1}{2} = \frac{}{2}$ $\qquad 6\frac{5}{7} = \frac{}{7}$

$\frac{11}{8} =$ _____ $\qquad \frac{21}{4} =$ _____ $\qquad \frac{33}{5} =$ _____ $\qquad \frac{13}{6} =$ _____

# Mix and Match

When adding mixed numbers, add the fractions first, then the whole numbers.

Examples:

$$9\frac{1}{3}$$
$$+3\frac{1}{3}$$
$$\overline{12\frac{2}{3}}$$

$$2\frac{3}{6}$$
$$+1\frac{1}{6}$$
$$\overline{3\frac{4}{6}}$$

**Directions:** Add the number in the center to the number in each surrounding section.

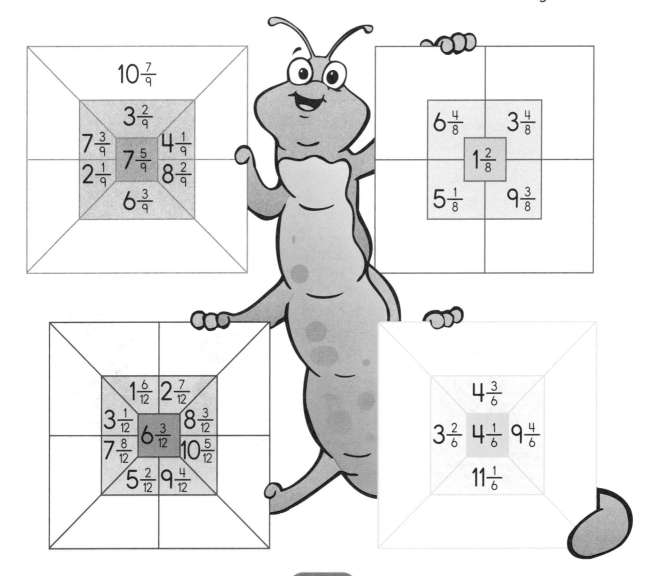

Name _____

# Mixed Up Math

When subtracting mixed numbers, subtract the fractions first, then the whole numbers.

**Directions:** Subtract the mixed numbers. The first one is done for you.

$$7\frac{3}{8} - 4\frac{2}{8} = 3\frac{1}{8}$$

$$4\frac{5}{6} - 3\frac{1}{6}$$

$$4\frac{1}{2} - 3$$

$$7\frac{5}{8} - 6\frac{3}{8}$$

$$6\frac{6}{8} - 1\frac{1}{8}$$

$$5\frac{2}{3} - 3\frac{1}{3}$$

$$4\frac{8}{10} - 3\frac{3}{10}$$

$$9\frac{8}{9} - 4\frac{3}{9}$$

$$7\frac{2}{3} - 6\frac{1}{3}$$

$$7\frac{2}{3} - 5$$

$$4\frac{7}{9} - 2$$

$$6\frac{7}{8} - 5\frac{3}{8}$$

$$6\frac{3}{4} - 3\frac{1}{4}$$

$$5\frac{6}{7} - 3\frac{1}{7}$$

$$7\frac{6}{7} - 2\frac{4}{7}$$

Tessa needs $1\frac{3}{8}$ yards of cloth to make a dress.
She has $4\frac{5}{8}$ yards. How much cloth will be left over? _____

# Fill It Up!

**Directions:** Add or subtract. Remember to include the decimal point in your answers.

**Example:**

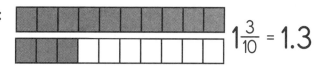

$1\frac{3}{10} = 1.3$

$1\frac{6}{10} = 1.6$

```
  1.3
+ 1.6
  2.9
```

| | | | | |
|---|---|---|---|---|
| 8.1 <br> + 1.7 | 4.1 <br> + 6.2 | 0.5 <br> + 1.6 | 7.6 <br> − 6.5 | 7.2 <br> − 2.6 |

| | | |
|---|---|---|
| 7.8 <br> − 6.8 | 16.5 <br> − 7.3 | 6.4 <br> + 5.3 |
| 0.42 <br> + 0.35 | 0.98 <br> − 0.87 | 0.78 <br> − 0.13 |
| 0.95 <br> − 0.14 | 3.23 <br> + 2.48 | 4.68 <br> − 2.65 |
| 6.98 <br> + 1.40 | 3.27 <br> + 1.82 | 4.65 <br> − 1.32 |

Mr. Martin went on a car trip with his family. Mr. Martin
purchased gas 3 times. He bought 6.7 gallons, 7.3 gallons,
then 5.8 gallons of gas. How much gas did he purchase in all? _____

# Rulers Rule

An inch is divided into smaller units, or fractions of an inch.

**Example:** This stick of gum is $2\frac{3}{4}$ inches long.

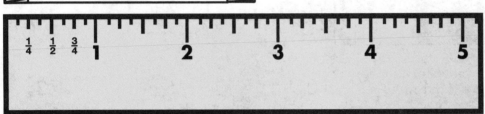

**Directions:** Use a ruler to measure each line to the nearest quarter of an inch. The first one is done for you.

1. $\frac{3}{4}$ inch _____ _____

2. _____ _____

3. _____

4. _____

5. _____

6. _____ _____

7. _____ _____

# Inside, Outside, All Around

**Perimeter** is the distance around a figure. It is found by adding the lengths of the sides. Area is also calculated by multiplying the length times the width of a square or rectangular figure. Use the formula: A = l x w.

**Directions:** Calculate the perimeter of each figure.

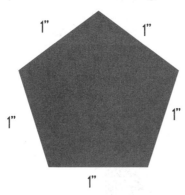

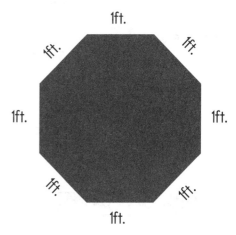

_____    _____    _____

**Directions:** Calculate the area of each figure.

_____    _____    _____

# Taking Up Space

The **volume** of a figure can be calculated by multiplying the length times the width times the height.

Use the formula: $V = l \times w \times h$.

**Example:**

$3 \times 5 \times 2 = 30$ cubic feet

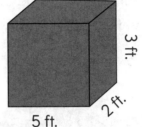

**Directions:** Find the volume of the following figures. Label your answers in cubic feet, inches, or yards. The first one is done for you.

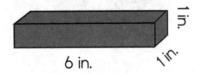

<u>6 cubic inches</u>

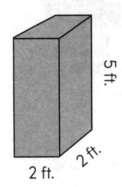

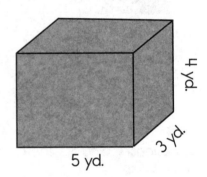

_____    _____

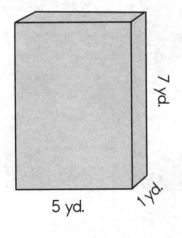

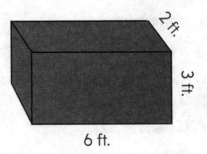

_____    _____

# Get Organized!

A **graph** is a drawing that shows information about changes in numbers.

**Directions:** Answer the questions by reading the graphs.

## Bar Graph

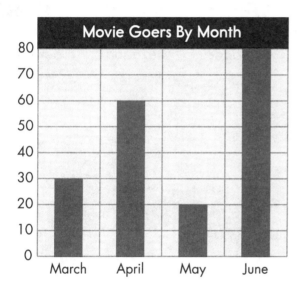

How many people went to see a movie in June?

_____

In which month did the fewest people go see a movie?

_____

How many total people went to see a movie in 4 months?

_____

## Line Graph

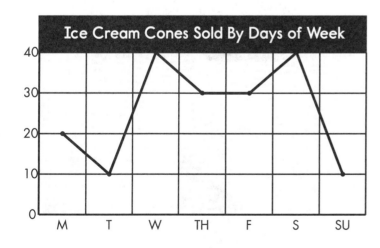

On which days did the store sell the fewest ice cream cones?

_____

How many ice cream cones did the store sell in 1 week?

_____

Name _____

# Picture a Polygon

A **polygon** is a closed figure with three or more sides.

**Examples:**

| triangle | square | rectangle | pentagon | hexagon | octagon |
| 3 sides | 4 equal sides | 4 sides | 5 sides | 6 sides | 8 sides |

**Directions:** Identify the polygons.

_____

_____

_____

_____

_____

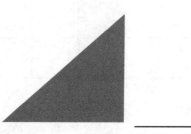

_____

# Get in Line!

A **line segment** has two end points.

Write:  AB

A **line** has no end points and goes on in both directions.

Write:  CD

A **ray** is part of a line and goes on in one direction. It has one end point.

Write:  EF

**Directions:** Identify each of the following as a line, line segment, or ray.

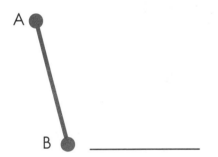

_____

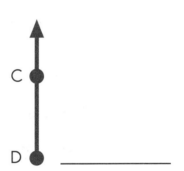

_____

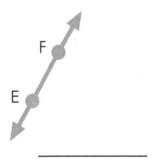

_____

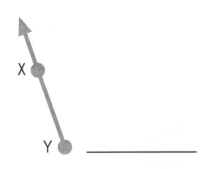

_____

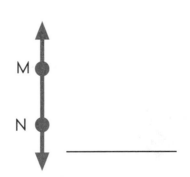

_____

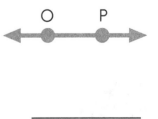

_____

# Angle Wrangler

The point at which two line segments meet is called an **angle**. There are three types of angles — right, acute, and obtuse.

 A **right angle** is formed when the two lines meet at 90°.

 An **acute angle** is formed when the two lines meet at less than 90°.

 An **obtuse angle** is formed when the two lines meet at greater than 90°.

Angles can be measured with a protractor or index card. With a protractor, align the bottom edge of the angle with the bottom of the protractor, with the angle point at the circle of the protractor. Note the direction of the other ray and the number of degrees of the angle.

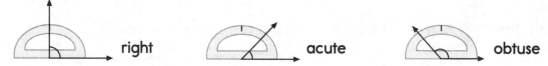

Place the corner of an index card in the corner of the angle. If the edges line up with the card, it is a right angle. If not, the angle is acute or obtuse.

**Directions:** Use a protractor or index card to identify the following angles as right, obtuse or acute.

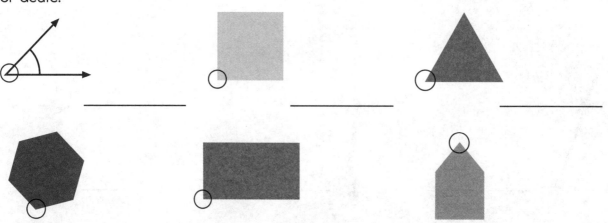

_____     _____     _____

_____     _____     _____

# Send in the Circles

A **circle** is a round figure. It is named by its center. A **radius** is a line segment from the center of a circle to any point on the circle. A **diameter** is a line segment with both end points on the circle. The diameter always passes through the center of the circle.

**Directions:** Name the radius, diameter and circle.

**Example:**

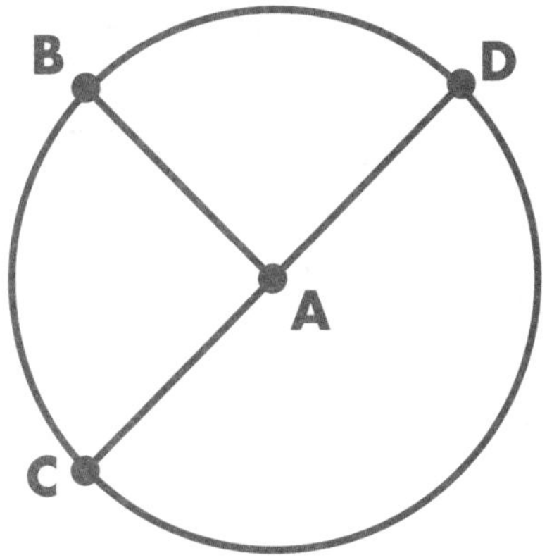

Circle _____A_____
Radius _____AB_____
Diameter _____DC_____

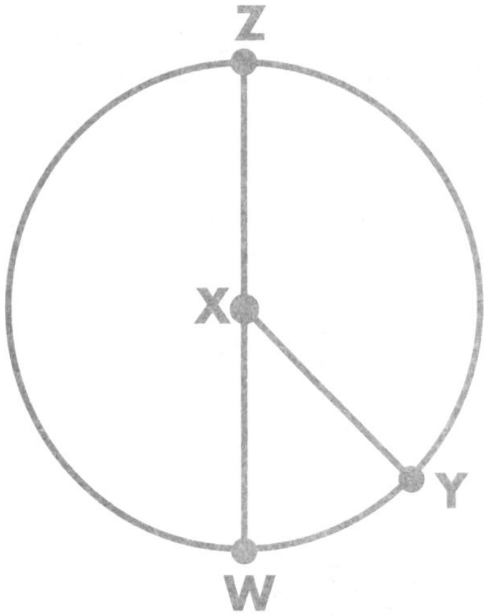

Circle _____
Radius _____
Diameter _____

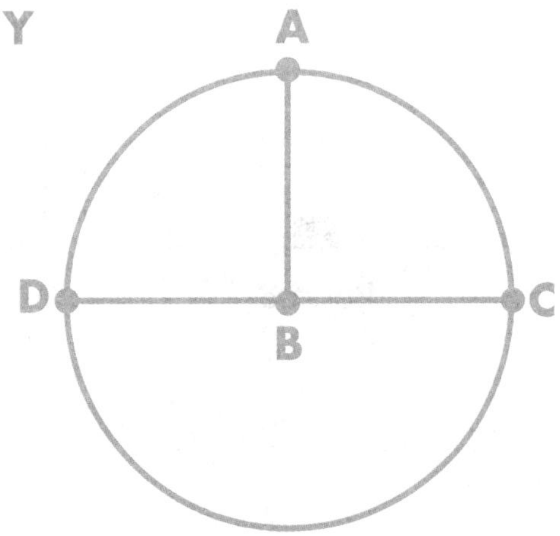

Circle _____
Radius _____
Diameter _____

## Page 4

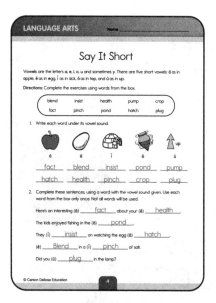

**Say It Short**

Vowels are the letters a, e, i, o, u and sometimes y. There are five short vowels: ă as in apple, ĕ as in egg, ĭ as in sick, ŏ as in top, and ŭ as in up.

Directions: Complete the exercises using words from the box.

| blend | insist | health | pump | crop |
| fact | pinch | pond | hatch | plug |

1. Write each word under its vowel sound.

ă: fact, blend, hatch, health
ĕ: insist, pinch
ĭ: pond, crop
ŏ: pump, plug

2. Complete these sentences, using a word with the vowel sound given. Use each word from the box only once. Not all words will be used.

Here's an interesting (ă) __fact__ about your (ĕ) __health__.
The kids went fishing in the (ŏ) __pond__.
They (ĭ) __insist__ on watching the egg (ă) __hatch__.
(ă) __Blend__ in a (ĭ) __pinch__ of salt.
Did you (ŭ) __plug__ in the lamp?

## Page 5

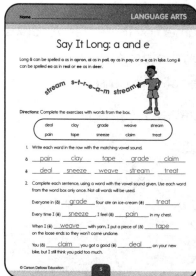

**Say It Long: a and e**

Long ā can be spelled a as in apron, ai as in pail, ay as in pay, or a-e as in lake. Long ē can be spelled ea as in real or ee as in deer.

stream  s-t-r-e-a-m  stream

Directions: Complete the exercises with words from the box.

| deal | clay | grade | weave | stream |
| pain | tape | sneeze | claim | treat |

1. Write each word in the row with the matching vowel sound.

ā: pain, clay, tape, grade, claim
ē: deal, sneeze, weave, stream, treat

2. Complete each sentence, using a word with the vowel sound given. Use each word from the word box only once. Not all words will be used.

Everyone in (ā) __grade__ four ate an ice-cream (ē) __treat__.
Every time I (ē) __sneeze__, I feel (ā) __pain__ in my chest.
When I (ā) __weave__ with yarn, I put a piece of (ā) __tape__ on the loose ends so they won't come undone.
You (ā) __claim__ you got a good (ē) __deal__ on your new bike, but I still think you paid too much.

## Page 6

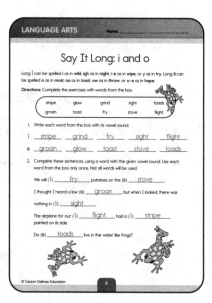

**Say It Long: i and o**

Long ī can be spelled i as in wild, igh as in night, i-e as in wipe, or y as in try. Long ō can be spelled o as in most, oa as in toast, ow as in throw, or o-e as in hope.

Directions: Complete the exercises with words from the box.

| stripe | glow | grind | sight | toads |
| groan | toast | fry | stove | flight |

1. Write each word from the box with its vowel sound.

ī: stripe, grind, fry, sight, flight
ō: groan, glow, toast, stove, toads

2. Complete these sentences, using a word with the given vowel sound. Use each word from the box only once. Not all words will be used.

We will (ī) __fry__ potatoes on the (ō) __stove__.
I thought I heard a low (ō) __groan__, but when I looked, there was nothing in (ī) __sight__.
The airplane for our (ī) __flight__ had a (ī) __stripe__ painted on its side.
Do (ō) __toads__ live in the water like frogs?

## Page 7

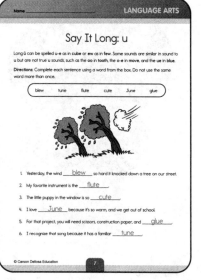

**Say It Long: u**

Long ū can be spelled u-e as in cube or ew as in few. Some sounds are similar in sound to u but are not true u sounds, such as the oo in tooth, the o-e in move, and the ue in blue.

Directions: Complete each sentence using a word from the box. Do not use the same word more than once.

| blew | tune | flute | cute | June | glue |

1. Yesterday, the wind __blew__ so hard it knocked down a tree on our street.
2. My favorite instrument is the __flute__.
3. The little puppy in the window is so __cute__.
4. I love __June__ because it's so warm, and we get out of school.
5. For that project, you will need scissors, construction paper, and __glue__.
6. I recognize that song because it has a familiar __tune__.

## Page 8

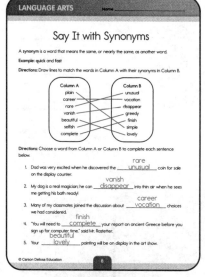

**Say It with Synonyms**

A synonym is a word that means the same, or nearly the same, as another word.

Example: quick and fast

Directions: Draw lines to match the words in Column A with their synonyms in Column B.

Column A: plain, career, rare, vanish, beautiful, selfish, complete
Column B: unusual, vocation, disappear, greedy, finish, simple, lovely

Directions: Choose a word from Column A or Column B to complete each sentence below.

1. Dad was very excited when he discovered the __rare/unusual__ coin for sale on the display counter.
2. My dog is a real magician; he can __vanish/disappear__ into thin air when he sees me getting his bath ready!
3. Many of my classmates joined the discussion about __career/vocation__ choices we had considered.
4. "You will need to __finish/complete__ your report on ancient Greece before you sign up for computer time," said Mr. Rostetter.
5. Your __beautiful/lovely__ painting will be on display in the art show.

## Page 9

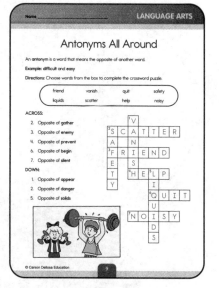

**Antonyms All Around**

An antonym is a word that means the opposite of another word.

Example: difficult and easy

Directions: Choose words from the box to complete the crossword puzzle.

| friend | vanish | quit | safety |
| liquids | scatter | help | noisy |

ACROSS:
2. Opposite of gather
3. Opposite of enemy
4. Opposite of prevent
6. Opposite of begin
7. Opposite of silent

DOWN:
1. Opposite of appear
2. Opposite of danger
5. Opposite of solids

Crossword answers: SCATTER, FRIEND, HELP, QUIT, NOISY, VANISH, SAFETY, LIQUIDS

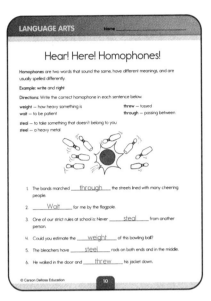

**Page 10**

LANGUAGE ARTS  Name

### Hear! Here! Homophones!

**Homophones** are two words that sound the same, have different meanings, and are usually spelled differently.

**Example:** write and right

**Directions:** Write the correct homophone in each sentence below.

weight — how heavy something is
wait — to be patient
steal — to take something that doesn't belong to you
steel — a heavy metal
threw — tossed
through — passing between

1. The bands marched ___through___ the streets lined with many cheering people.
2. ___Wait___ for me by the flagpole.
3. One of our strict rules at school is: Never ___steal___ from another person.
4. Could you estimate the ___weight___ of this bowling ball?
5. The bleachers have ___steel___ rods on both ends and in the middle.
6. He walked in the door and ___threw___ his jacket down.

© Carson Dellosa Education    10

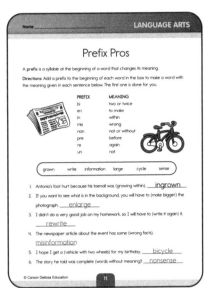

**Page 11**

Name    LANGUAGE ARTS

### Prefix Pros

A **prefix** is a syllable at the beginning of a word that changes its meaning.

**Directions:** Add a prefix to the beginning of each word in the box to make a word with the meaning given in each sentence below. The first one is done for you.

| PREFIX | MEANING |
| --- | --- |
| bi | two or twice |
| en | to make |
| in | within |
| mis | wrong |
| non | not or without |
| pre | before |
| re | again |
| un | not |

grown   write   information   large   cycle   sense

1. Antonio's foot hurt because his toenail was (growing within). ___ingrown___
2. If you want to see what is in the background, you will have to (make bigger) the photograph. ___enlarge___
3. I didn't do a very good job on my homework, so I will have to (write it again) it. ___rewrite___
4. The newspaper article about the event has some (wrong facts). ___misinformation___
5. I hope I get a (vehicle with two wheels) for my birthday. ___bicycle___
6. The story he told was complete (words without meaning)! ___nonsense___

© Carson Dellosa Education    11

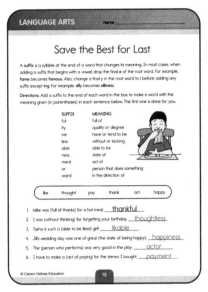

**Page 12**

LANGUAGE ARTS    Name

### Save the Best for Last

A **suffix** is a syllable at the end of a word that changes its meaning. In most cases, when adding a suffix that begins with a vowel, drop the final e of the root word. For example, **fame** becomes **famous**. Also, change a final y in the root word to i before adding any suffix except ing. For example, **silly** becomes **silliness**.

**Directions:** Add a suffix to the end of each word in the box to make a word with the meaning given (in parentheses) in each sentence below. The first one is done for you.

| SUFFIX | MEANING |
| --- | --- |
| ful | full of |
| ity | quality or degree |
| ive | have or tend to be |
| less | without or lacking |
| able | able to be |
| ness | state of |
| ment | act of |
| or | person that does something |
| ward | in the direction of |

like   thought   pay   thank   act   happy

1. Mike was (full of thanks) for a hot meal. ___thankful___
2. I was (without thinking) for forgetting your birthday. ___thoughtless___
3. Tasha is such a (able to be liked) girl! ___likable___
4. Jill's wedding day was one of great (the state of being happy). ___happiness___
5. The (person who performs) was very good in the play. ___actor___
6. I have to make a (act of paying) for the stereo I bought. ___payment___

© Carson Dellosa Education    12

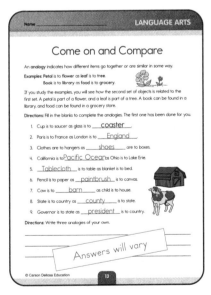

**Page 13**

Name    LANGUAGE ARTS

### Come on and Compare

An **analogy** indicates how different items go together or are similar in some way.

**Examples:** Petal is to flower as leaf is to tree.
Book is to library as food is to grocery.

If you study the examples, you will see how the second set of objects is related to the first set. A petal is part of a flower, and a leaf is part of a tree. A book can be found in a library, and food can be found in a grocery store.

**Directions:** Fill in the blanks to complete the analogies. The first one has been done for you.

1. Cup is to saucer as glass is to ___coaster___.
2. Paris is to France as London is to ___England___.
3. Clothes are to hangers as ___shoes___ are to boxes.
4. California is to ___Pacific Ocean___ as Ohio is to Lake Erie.
5. ___Tablecloth___ is to table as blanket is to bed.
6. Pencil is to paper as ___paintbrush___ is to canvas.
7. Cow is to ___barn___ as child is to house.
8. State is to country as ___county___ is to state.
9. Governor is to state as ___president___ is to country.

**Directions:** Write three analogies of your own.

___Answers will vary___

© Carson Dellosa Education    13

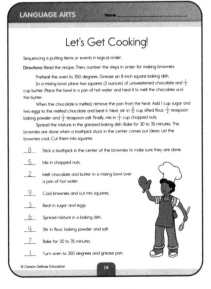

**Page 14**

LANGUAGE ARTS    Name

### Let's Get Cooking!

Sequencing is putting items or events in logical order.

**Directions:** Read the recipe. Then, number the steps in order for making brownies.

Preheat the oven to 350 degrees. Grease an 8-inch square baking dish.

In a mixing bowl, place two squares (2 ounces) of unsweetened chocolate and ¼ cup butter. Place the bowl in a pan of hot water and heat it to melt the chocolate and the butter.

When the chocolate is melted, remove the pan from the heat. Add 1 cup sugar and two eggs to the melted chocolate and beat it. Next, stir in ¼ cup sifted flour, ¼ teaspoon baking powder and ¼ teaspoon salt. Finally, mix in ¼ cup chopped nuts.

Spread the mixture in the greased baking dish. Bake for 30 to 35 minutes. The brownies are done when a toothpick stuck in the center comes out clean. Let the brownies cool. Cut them into squares.

___8___ Stick a toothpick in the center of the brownies to make sure they are done.
___5___ Mix in chopped nuts.
___2___ Melt chocolate and butter in a mixing bowl over a pan of hot water.
___9___ Cool brownies and cut into squares.
___3___ Beat in sugar and eggs.
___6___ Spread mixture in a baking dish.
___4___ Stir in flour, baking powder and salt.
___7___ Bake for 30 to 35 minutes.
___1___ Turn oven to 350 degrees and grease pan.

© Carson Dellosa Education    14

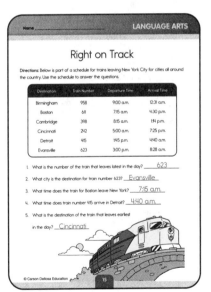

**Page 15**

Name    LANGUAGE ARTS

### Right on Track

**Directions:** Below is part of a schedule for trains leaving New York City for cities all around the country. Use the schedule to answer the questions.

| Destination | Train Number | Departure Time | Arrival Time |
| --- | --- | --- | --- |
| Birmingham | 958 | 9:00 a.m. | 12:31 p.m. |
| Boston | 611 | 7:15 a.m. | 4:30 p.m. |
| Cambridge | 398 | 8:15 a.m. | 1:14 p.m. |
| Cincinnati | 242 | 5:00 a.m. | 7:25 p.m. |
| Detroit | 415 | 1:45 p.m. | 4:40 a.m. |
| Evansville | 623 | 3:00 p.m. | 8:28 a.m. |

1. What is the number of the train that leaves latest in the day? ___623___
2. What city is the destination for train number 623? ___Evansville___
3. What time does the train for Boston leave New York? ___7:15 a.m.___
4. What time does train number 415 arrive in Detroit? ___4:40 a.m.___
5. What is the destination of the train that leaves earliest in the day? ___Cincinnati___

© Carson Dellosa Education    15

# ANSWER KEY

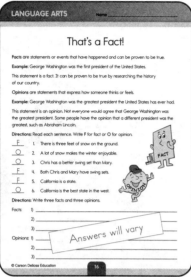

## Page 16 — That's a Fact!

**Facts** are statements or events that have happened and can be proven to be true.

**Example:** George Washington was the first president of the United States.

This statement is a fact. It can be proven to be true by researching the history of our country.

**Opinions** are statements that express how someone thinks or feels.

**Example:** George Washington was the greatest president the United States has ever had.

This statement is an opinion. Not everyone would agree that George Washington was the greatest president. Some people have the opinion that a different president was the greatest, such as Abraham Lincoln.

**Directions:** Read each sentence. Write F for fact or O for opinion.

F   1. There is three feet of snow on the ground.
O   2. A lot of snow makes the winter enjoyable.
O   3. Chris has a better swing set than Mary.
F   4. Both Chris and Mary have swing sets.
F   5. California is a state.
O   6. California is the best state in the west.

**Directions:** Write three facts and three opinions.

Facts: 1)
2)
3)

Opinions: 1)
2)
3)

*Answers will vary*

© Carson Dellosa Education    16

**Page 16**

## Page 17 — Get to the Point

The **main idea** is the most important idea, or main point, in a sentence, paragraph, or story.

**Directions:** Circle the main idea for each sentence.

1. Emily knew she would be late if she watched the end of the TV show.
   a. Emily likes watching TV.
   b. Emily is always running late.
   c. If Emily didn't leave, she would be late. *(circled)*

2. The dog was too strong and pulled Jason across the park with his leash.
   a. The dog is stronger than Jason. *(circled)*
   b. Jason is not very strong.
   c. Jason took the dog for a walk.

3. Jennifer took the book home so she could read it over and over.
   a. Jennifer loves to read.
   b. Jennifer loves the book. *(circled)*
   c. Jennifer is a good reader.

4. Jerome threw the baseball so hard it broke the window.
   a. Jerome throws baseballs very hard. *(circled)*
   b. Jerome was mad at the window.
   c. Jerome can't throw very straight.

5. Lori came home and decided to clean the kitchen for her parents.
   a. Lori is a very nice person.
   b. Lori did a favor for her parents. *(circled)*
   c. Lori likes to cook.

6. It was raining so hard that it was hard to see the road through the windshield.
   a. It always rains hard in April.
   b. The rain blurred our vision. *(circled)*
   c. It's hard to drive in the rain.

© Carson Dellosa Education    17

**Page 17**

## Page 18 — Winter Wonderland

The **main idea** of a story or report is a sentence that summarizes the most important point. If a story or report is only one paragraph in length, then the main idea is usually stated in the first sentence (topic sentence). If it is longer than one paragraph, then the main idea is a general sentence including all the important points of the story or report.

**Directions:** Read the story about snow fun. Then, draw an X in the blank for the main idea.

After a big snowfall, my friends and I enjoy playing in the snow. We bundle up in snow clothes at our homes, then meet with sleds at the hill by my house.

One by one, we take turns sledding down the hill to see who will go the farthest and the fastest. Sometimes we have a contest to see whose sled will reach the fence at the foot of the hill first.

When we tire of sledding, we may build a snowman or snowforts. Sometimes we have a friendly snowball fight.

The end of our snow fun comes too quickly, and we head home to warm houses, dry clothes, and hot chocolate.

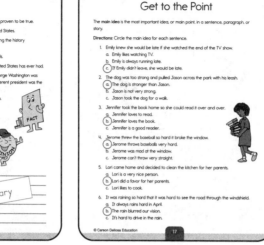

1. What is the main idea?
   X   Playing in the snow with friends is an enjoyable activity.
   ___ Sledding in the snow is fast and fun.

If you selected the first option, you are correct. The paragraphs discuss the enjoyable things friends do on a snowy day.

The second option is not correct because the entire story is not about sledding. Only the second paragraph discusses sledding. The other paragraphs discuss the additional ways friends have fun in the snow.

2. Write a paragraph about what you like to do ... member to make the first sentence.

*Paragraphs will vary*

© Carson Dellosa Education    18

**Page 18**

## Page 19 — Ask It, State It

A **statement** tells some kind of information. It is followed by a period (.).

**Examples:** It is a rainy day. We are going to the beach next summer.

A **question** asks for a specific piece of information. It is followed by a question mark (?).

**Examples:** What is the weather like today? When are you going to the beach?

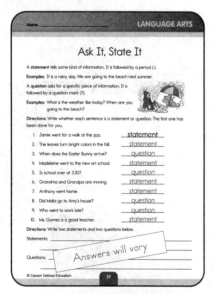

**Directions:** Write whether each sentence is a statement or question. The first one has been done for you.

1. Jamie went for a walk at the zoo.    statement
2. The leaves turn bright colors in the fall.    statement
3. When does the Easter Bunny arrive?    question
4. Madeleine went to the new art school.    statement
5. Is school over at 3:30?    question
6. Grandma and Grandpa are moving.    statement
7. Anthony went home.    statement
8. Did Malia go to Amy's house?    question
9. Who went to work late?    question
10. Ms. Gomez is a good teacher.    statement

**Directions:** Write two statements and two questions below.

Statements:

Questions:

*Answers will vary*

© Carson Dellosa Education    19

**Page 19**

## Page 20 — Taking Command

A **command** tells someone to do something. It is followed by a period (.).

**Examples:** Get your math book. Do your homework.

An **exclamation** shows strong feeling or excitement. It is followed by an exclamation mark (!).

**Examples:** Watch out for that car! Oh, no! There's a snake!

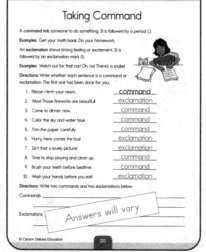

**Directions:** Write whether each sentence is a command or exclamation. The first one has been done for you.

1. Please clean your room.    command
2. Wow! Those fireworks are beautiful.    exclamation
3. Come to dinner now.    command
4. Color the sky and water blue.    command
5. Trim the paper carefully.    command
6. Hurry, here comes the bus!    exclamation
7. Isn't that a lovely picture!    exclamation
8. Time to stop playing and clean up.    command
9. Brush your teeth before bedtime.    command
10. Wash your hands before you eat!    exclamation

**Directions:** Write two commands and two exclamations below.

Commands:

Exclamations:

*Answers will vary*

© Carson Dellosa Education    20

**Page 20**

## Page 21 — Subject Matters

The **subject** of a sentence tells you who or what the sentence is about. A subject is either a common noun, a proper noun, or a pronoun.

**Examples:** I went to the store. I is the subject of the sentence.
The tired boys and girls walked home slowly.
**The tired boys and girls** is the subject of the sentence.

**Directions:** Underline the subject of each sentence. The first one has been done for you.

1. The birthday cake was pink and white.
2. Anthony celebrated his fourth birthday.
3. The tower of building blocks fell over.
4. On Saturday, our family will go to a movie.
5. The busy editor was writing sentences.
6. Seven children painted pictures.
7. Two happy dolphins played cheerfully on the surf.
8. A sand crab buried itself in the dunes.

**Directions:** Write a subject for each sentence.

1. Chocolate-chip ice cream was melting in the heat.
2. ___ ran down ...
3. ___
4. ___
5. ___ made her a beautiful dress.
6. ___ hopped, skipped, and jumped all the way home.

*Answers will vary*

© Carson Dellosa Education    21

**Page 21**

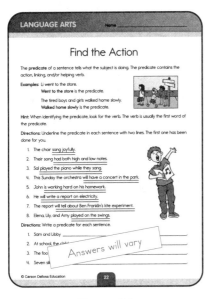

**Page 22**

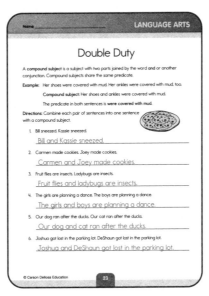

**Page 23**

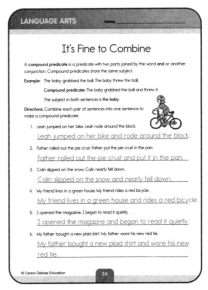

**Page 24**

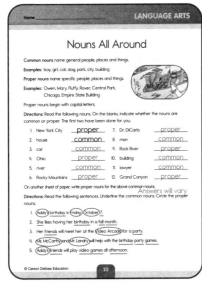

**Page 25**

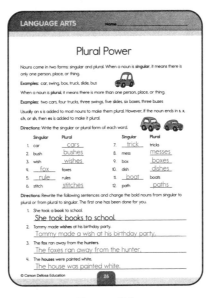

**Page 26**

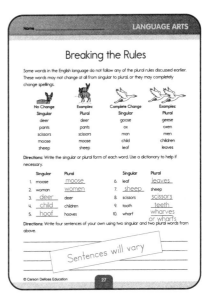

**Page 27**

## Pronoun Lowdown

A **pronoun** is a word that takes the place of a noun in a sentence.

**Examples:** I, my, mine, me
we, our, ours, us
you, your, yours
he, his, him
she, her, hers
it, its
they, their, theirs, them

**Directions:** Underline the pronouns in each sentence.

1. Bring them to us as soon as you are finished.
2. She has been my best friend for many years.
3. They should be here soon.
4. We enjoyed our trip to the Mustard Museum.
5. Would you be able to help us with the project on Saturday?
6. Our homeroom teacher will not be here tomorrow.
7. My uncle said that he will be leaving soon for Australia.
8. Hurry! Could you please open the door for him?

© Carson Dellosa Education    28

**Page 28**

## Verb Alert

Verbs show action or state of being. There are three kinds of verbs: action verbs, linking verbs, and helping verbs.

An **action verb** tells the action of a sentence.

**Examples:** run, hop, skip, sleep, jump, talk, snore
Michael ran to the store. Ran is the action verb.

A **linking verb** joins the subject and predicate of a sentence.

**Examples:** am, is, are, was, were
Michael was at the store. Was is the linking verb.

A **helping verb** is used with an action or linking verb to "help" express the subject's action or state of being.

**Examples:** am, is, are, was, were
Matthew was helping Michael. Was helps the action verb helping.

**Directions:** Read the following sentences. Underline the verbs. Above each, write A for action verb, L for linking verb, or H for helping verb. The first one has been done for you.

1. Amy jumps rope. (A)
2. Kahlil was jumping rope, too. (H A)
3. They were working on their homework. (H A)
4. The math problem requires a lot of thinking. (A)
5. Addition problems are fun to do. (L)
6. The baby sleeps in the afternoon. (A)
7. Grandma is napping also. (H A)
8. Sam is going to bed. (H A)
9. Jackson paints a lovely picture of the sea. (A)
10. The colors in the picture are soft and pale. (L)

© Carson Dellosa Education    29

**Page 29**

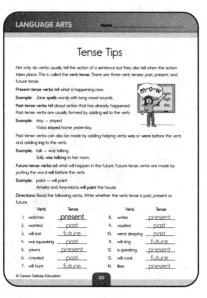

## Tense Tips

Not only do verbs usually tell the action of a sentence but they also tell when the action takes place. This is called the **verb tense**. There are three verb tenses: past, present, and future tense.

**Present-tense verbs** tell what is happening now.
**Example:** Jane spells words with long vowel sounds.
**Past-tense verbs** tell about action that has already happened.
Past-tense verbs are usually formed by adding **ed** to the verb.
**Example:** stay — stayed
Vidas stayed home yesterday.

Past-tense verbs can also be made by adding helping verbs was or were before the verb and adding ing to the verb.
**Example:** talk — was talking
Sally was talking to her mom.
**Future-tense verbs** tell what will happen in the future. Future-tense verbs are made by putting the word will before the verb.
**Example:** paint — will paint
Amelia and Ana-Maria will paint the house.

**Directions:** Read the following verbs. Write whether the verb tense is past, present, or future.

| | Verb | Tense | | Verb | Tense |
|---|---|---|---|---|---|
| 1. | watches | present | 8. | writes | present |
| 2. | wanted | past | 9. | vaulted | past |
| 3. | will eat | future | 10. | were sleeping | past |
| 4. | was squawking | past | 11. | will sing | future |
| 5. | yawns | present | 12. | is speaking | present |
| 6. | crawled | past | 13. | will cook | future |
| 7. | will hunt | future | 14. | likes | present |

© Carson Dellosa Education    30

**Page 30**

## That's History!

**Irregular verbs** change completely in the past tense. Unlike regular verbs, past-tense forms of irregular verbs are not formed by adding ed.

**Example:** The past tense of go is went.
Other verbs change some letters to form the past tense.
**Example:** The past tense of break is broke.

A **helping verb** helps to tell about the past. Has, have, and had are helping verbs used with action verbs to show the action occurred in the past. The past-tense form of the irregular verb sometimes changes when a helping verb is added.

| Present Tense Irregular Verb | Past Tense Irregular Verb | Past Tense Irregular Verb With Helper |
|---|---|---|
| go | went | have/has/had gone |
| see | saw | have/has/had seen |
| do | did | have/has/had done |
| bring | brought | have/has/had brought |
| sing | sang | have/has/had sung |
| drive | drove | have/has/had driven |
| swim | swam | have/has/had swum |
| sleep | slept | have/has/had slept |

**Directions:** Choose four words from the chart. Write one sentence using the past-tense form of the verb without a helping verb. Write another sentence using the past-tense form with a helping verb.

1. _Sentences will vary_
2.
3.
4.

© Carson Dellosa Education    31

**Page 31**

## Prescription for Description

Adjectives tell more about nouns. Adjectives are describing words.

**Examples:** scary animals    bright glow    wet frog

**Directions:** Add at least two adjectives to each sentence below. Use your own words or words from the box.

| | | | | | |
|---|---|---|---|---|---|
| pale | soft | sticky | burning | furry | glistening | peaceful |
| faint | shivering | slippery | gleaming | gentle | foggy | tangled |

**Example:** The stripe was blue.
The wide stripe was light blue.

1. The frog had eyes.
2. The house was a sight.
3. A boy heard a noise.
4. The girl _Sentences will vary_
5. A tiger ran through the room.
6. They saw a glow in the window.

© Carson Dellosa Education    32

**Page 32**

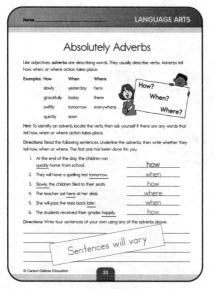

## Absolutely Adverbs

Like adjectives, **adverbs** are describing words. They usually describe verbs. Adverbs tell how, when, or where action takes place.

| How | When | Where |
|---|---|---|
| slowly | yesterday | here |
| gracefully | today | there |
| swiftly | tomorrow | everywhere |
| quickly | soon | |

**Hint:** To identify an adverb, locate the verb, then ask yourself if there are any words that tell how, when, or where action takes place.

**Directions:** Read the following sentences. Underline the adverbs, then write whether they tell how, when, or where. The first one has been done for you.

1. At the end of the day, the children ran quickly home from school. — how
2. They will have a spelling test tomorrow. — when
3. Slowly, the children filed to their seats. — how
4. The teacher sat here at her desk. — where
5. She will pass the tests back later. — when
6. The students received their grades happily. — how

**Directions:** Write four sentences of your own using any of the adverbs above.

_Sentences will vary_

© Carson Dellosa Education    33

**Page 33**

## Page 34

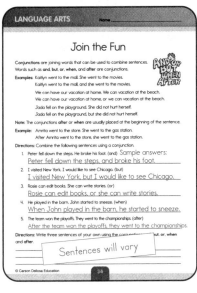

**LANGUAGE ARTS**    Name _____

### Join the Fun

Conjunctions are joining words that can be used to combine sentences. Words such as **and, but, or, when,** and **after** are conjunctions.

**Examples:** Kaitlyn went to the mall. She went to the movies.
Kaitlyn went to the mall, and she went to the movies.

We can have our vacation at home. We can vacation at the beach.
We can have our vacation at home, or we can vacation at the beach.

Jada fell on the playground. She did not hurt herself.
Jada fell on the playground, but she did not hurt herself.

**Note:** The conjunctions **after** or **when** are usually placed at the beginning of the sentence.

**Example:** Amrita went to the store. She went to the gas station.
After Amrita went to the store, she went to the gas station.

**Directions:** Combine the following sentences using a conjunction.

1. Peter fell down the steps. He broke his foot. (and) *Sample answers:*
   Peter fell down the steps, and broke his foot.
2. I visited New York. I would like to see Chicago. (but)
   I visited New York, but I would like to see Chicago.
3. Rosie can edit books. She can write stories. (or)
   Rosie can edit books, or she can write stories.
4. He played in the barn. John started to sneeze. (when)
   When John played in the barn, he started to sneeze.
5. The team won the playoffs. They went to the championships. (after)
   After the team won the playoffs, they went to the championships.

**Directions:** Write three sentences of your own using the conjunctions but, or, when and after.

Sentences will vary

© Carson Dellosa Education   34

## Page 35

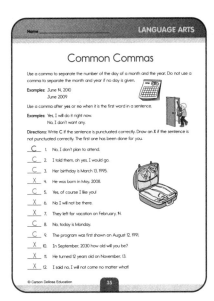

Name _____    **LANGUAGE ARTS**

### Common Commas

Use a comma to separate the number of the day of a month and the year. Do not use a comma to separate the month and year if no day is given.

**Examples:** June 14, 2010
June 2009

Use a comma after **yes** or **no** when it is the first word in a sentence.

**Examples:** Yes, I will do it right now.
No, I don't want any.

**Directions:** Write C if the sentence is punctuated correctly. Draw an X if the sentence is not punctuated correctly. The first one has been done for you.

- C 1. No, I don't plan to attend.
- C 2. I told them, oh yes, I would go.
- C 3. Her birthday is March 13, 1995.
- X 4. He was born in May, 2008.
- C 5. Yes, of course I like you!
- X 6. No I will not be there.
- X 7. They left for vacation on February, 14.
- C 8. No, today is Monday.
- C 9. The program was first shown on August 12, 1991.
- X 10. In September, 2030 how old will you be?
- X 11. He turned 12 years old on November, 13.
- X 12. I said no, I will not come no matter what!

© Carson Dellosa Education   35

## Page 36

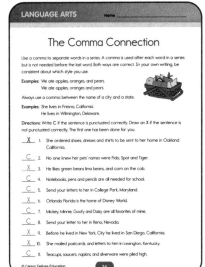

**LANGUAGE ARTS**    Name _____

### The Comma Connection

Use a comma to separate words in a series. A comma is used after each word in a series but is not needed before the last word. Both ways are correct. In your own writing, be consistent about which style you use.

**Examples:** We ate apples, oranges, and pears.
We ate apples, oranges and pears.

Always use a comma between the name of a city and a state.

**Examples:** She lives in Fresno, California.
He lives in Wilmington, Delaware.

**Directions:** Write C if the sentence is punctuated correctly. Draw an X if the sentence is not punctuated correctly. The first one has been done for you.

- X 1. She ordered shoes, dresses and shirts to be sent to her home in Oakland California.
- C 2. No one knew her pets' names were Fido, Spot and Tiger.
- X 3. He likes green beans lima beans, and corn on the cob.
- C 4. Notebooks, pens and pencils are all needed for school.
- C 5. Send your letters to her in College Park, Maryland.
- X 6. Orlando Florida is the home of Disney World.
- C 7. Mickey, Minnie, Goofy and Daisy are all favorites of mine.
- C 8. Send your letter to her in Reno, Nevada.
- X 9. Before he lived in New York, City he lived in San Diego, California.
- X 10. She mailed postcards, and letters to him in Lexington, Kentucky.
- C 11. Teacups, saucers, napkins and silverware were piled high.

© Carson Dellosa Education   36

## Page 37

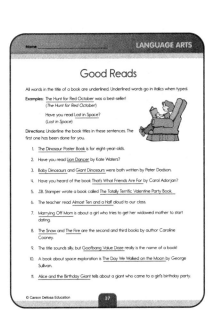

Name _____    **LANGUAGE ARTS**

### Good Reads

All words in the title of a book are underlined. Underlined words go in italics when typed.

**Examples:** The Hunt for Red October was a best-seller!
(The Hunt for Red October)

Have you read Lost in Space?
(Lost in Space)

**Directions:** Underline the book titles in these sentences. The first one has been done for you.

1. The Dinosaur Poster Book is for eight-year-olds.
2. Have you read Lion Dancer by Kate Waters?
3. Baby Dinosaurs and Giant Dinosaurs were both written by Peter Dodson.
4. Have you heard of the book That's What Friends Are For by Carol Adorjan?
5. J.B. Stamper wrote a book called The Totally Terrific Valentine Party Book.
6. The teacher read Almost Ten and a Half aloud to our class.
7. Marrying Off Mom is about a girl who tries to get her widowed mother to start dating.
8. The Snow and The Fire are the second and third books by author Caroline Cooney.
9. The title sounds silly, but Goofbang Value Daze really is the name of a book!
10. A book about space exploration is The Day We Walked on the Moon by George Sullivan.
11. Alice and the Birthday Giant tells about a giant who came to a girl's birthday party.

© Carson Dellosa Education   37

## Page 38

**LANGUAGE ARTS**    Name _____

### You Said It!

Use quotation marks (" ") before and after the exact words of a speaker.

**Examples:** I asked Aunt Martha, "How do you feel?"
"I feel awful," Aunt Martha replied.

Do not put quotation marks around words that report what the speaker said.

**Examples:** Aunt Martha said she felt awful.
I asked Aunt Martha how she felt.

**Directions:** Write C if the sentence is punctuated correctly. Draw an X if the sentence is not punctuated correctly. The first one has been done for you.

- C 1. "I want it right now!" she demanded angrily.
- X 2. "Do you want it now? I asked."
- X 3. She said "she felt better" now.
- C 4. Her exact words were, "I feel much better now!"
- C 5. "I am so thrilled to be here!" he shouted.
- C 6. "Yes, I will attend," she replied.
- X 7. Elizabeth said "she was unhappy."
- C 8. "I'm unhappy," Elizabeth reported.
- C 9. "Did you know her mother?" I asked.
- X 10. I asked "whether you knew her mother."
- C 11. I wondered, "What will dessert be?"
- C 12. "Which will it be, salt or pepper?" the waiter asked.

© Carson Dellosa Education   38

## Page 39

Name _____    **LANGUAGE ARTS**

### On the Run

A **run-on** sentence occurs when two or more sentences are joined together without punctuation.

**Examples:** Run-on sentence: I lost my way once did you?
Two sentences with correct punctuation: I lost my way once. Did you?
Run-on sentence: I found the recipe it was not hard to follow.
Two sentences with correct punctuation: I found the recipe. It was not hard to follow.

**Directions:** Rewrite the run-on sentences correctly with periods, exclamation points, and question marks. The first one has been done for you.

1. Did you take my umbrella I can't find it anywhere!
   Did you take my umbrella? I can't find it anywhere!
2. How can you stand that noise I can't!
   How can you stand that noise? I can't!
3. The cookies are gone I see only crumbs.
   The cookies are gone. I see only crumbs.
4. The dogs were barking they were hungry.
   The dogs were barking. They were hungry.
5. She is quite ill please call a doctor immediately!
   She is quite ill. Please call the doctor immediately!
6. The clouds came up we knew the storm would hit soon.
   The clouds came up. We knew the storm would hit soon.
7. You weren't home he stopped by this morning.
   You weren't home. He stopped by this morning.

© Carson Dellosa Education   39

# ANSWER KEY

**Page 40**

**LANGUAGE ARTS** — Name _____

## Putting It Together

**Directions:** Make each pair of sentences into one sentence. (You may have to change the verbs for some sentences—from is to are, for example.)

**Example:** Our house was flooded. Our car was flooded.

Our house and car were flooded.

1. Dmitry sees a glow.     Carrie sees a glow.
   Dmitry and Carrie see a glow.

2. Our new stove came today.     Our new refrigerator came today.
   Our new stove and refrigerator came today.

3. The pond is full of toads.     The field is full of toads.
   The pond and field are full of toads.

4. Stripes are on the flag.     Stars are on the flag.
   Stripes and stars are on the flag.

5. The ducks took flight.     The geese took flight.
   The ducks and geese took flight.

6. Joe reads stories.     Dana reads stories.
   Joe and Dana read stories.

© Carson Dellosa Education — 40

---

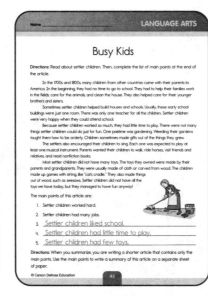

**Page 41**

Name _____ — **LANGUAGE ARTS**

## Busy Kids

**Directions:** Read about settler children. Then, complete the list of main points at the end of the article.

In the 1700s and 1800s, many children from other countries came with their parents to America. In the beginning, they had no time to go to school. They had to help their families work in the fields, care for the animals, and clean the house. They also helped care for their younger brothers and sisters.

Sometimes settler children helped build houses and schools. Usually, these early school buildings were just one room. There was only one teacher for all the children. Settler children were very happy when they could attend school.

Because settler children worked so much, they had little time to play. There were not many things settler children could do just for fun. One pastime was gardening. Weeding their gardens taught them how to be orderly. Children sometimes made gifts out of the things they grew.

The settlers also encouraged their children to sing. Each one was expected to play at least one musical instrument. Parents wanted their children to walk, ride horses, visit friends and relatives, and read nonfiction books.

Most settler children did not have many toys. The toys they owned were made by their parents and grandparents. They were usually made of cloth or carved from wood. The children made up games with string, like "cat's cradle." They also made things out of wood, such as seesaws. Settler children did not have all the toys we have today, but they managed to have fun anyway!

The main points of this article are:

1. Settler children worked hard.
2. Settler children had many jobs.
3. Settler children liked school.
4. Settler children had little time to play.
5. Settler children had few toys.

**Directions:** When you summarize, you are writing a shorter article that contains only the main points. Use the main points to write a summary of this article on a separate sheet of paper.

© Carson Dellosa Education — 41

---

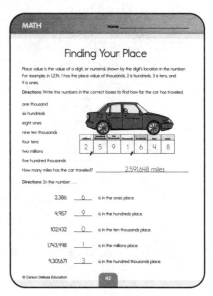

**Page 42**

**MATH** — Name _____

## Finding Your Place

Place value is the value of a digit, or numeral, shown by the digit's location in the number. For example, in 1,234, 1 has the place value of thousands, 2 is hundreds, 3 is tens, and 4 is ones.

**Directions:** Write the numbers in the correct boxes to find how far the car has traveled.

one thousand
six hundreds
eight ones
nine ten thousands
four tens
two millions
five hundred thousands

| millions | hundred thousands | ten thousands | thousands | hundreds | tens | ones |
|---|---|---|---|---|---|---|
| 2 | 5 | 9 | 1 | 6 | 4 | 8 |

How many miles has the car traveled?     2,591,648 miles

**Directions:** In the number . . .

2,386 — **6** — is in the ones place.

4,957 — **9** — is in the hundreds place.

1,024,432 — **0** — is in the ten thousands place.

1,743,998 — **1** — is in the millions place.

9,301,671 — **3** — is in the hundred thousands place.

© Carson Dellosa Education — 42

---

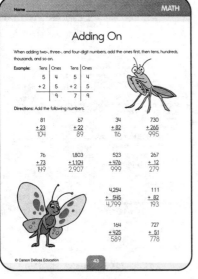

**Page 43**

Name _____ — **MATH**

## Adding On

When adding two-, three-, and four-digit numbers, add the ones first, then tens, hundreds, thousands, and so on.

**Example:**

| Tens | Ones |   | Tens | Ones |
|---|---|---|---|---|
| 5 | 4 |   | 5 | 4 |
| +2 | 5 |   | +2 | 5 |
|   | 9 |   | 7 | 9 |

**Directions:** Add the following numbers.

81 + 23 = 104       67 + 22 = 89       34 + 82 = 116       730 + 265 = 995

76 + 73 = 149       1,803 + 1,104 = 2,907       523 + 476 = 999       267 + 12 = 279

4,254 + 545 = 4,799       111 + 82 = 193

164 + 425 = 589       727 + 51 = 778

© Carson Dellosa Education — 43

---

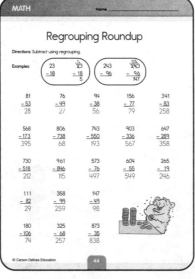

**Page 44**

**MATH** — Name _____

## Regrouping Roundup

**Directions:** Subtract using regrouping.

**Examples:**

23 − 18 = 5       243 − 96 = 147

81 − 53 = 28       76 − 49 = 27       94 − 38 = 56       156 − 77 = 79       341 − 83 = 258

568 − 173 = 395       806 − 738 = 68       743 − 550 = 193       903 − 336 = 567       647 − 289 = 358

730 − 518 = 212       961 − 846 = 115       573 − 76 = 497       604 − 55 = 549       265 − 19 = 246

111 − 82 = 29       358 − 99 = 259       147 − 49 = 98

180 − 106 = 74       325 − 68 = 257       873 − 35 = 838

© Carson Dellosa Education — 44

---

**Page 45**

Name _____ — **MATH**

## Round Up, Round Down

When rounding to the nearest hundred, the key number is in the tens place. If the tens digit is 5 or larger, round up to the nearest hundred. If the tens digit is 4 or less, round down to the nearest hundred.

**Examples:**

Round 871 to the nearest hundred.
7 is the key digit.
If it is more than 5, round up.
**Answer: 900**

Round 421 to the nearest hundred.
2 is the key digit.
If it is less than 5, round down.
**Answer: 400**

**Directions:** Round these numbers to the nearest hundred.

255 — **300**       368 — **400**       443 — **400**

562 — **600**       698 — **700**       99 — **100**

812 — **800**       592 — **600**       124 — **100**

When rounding to the nearest thousand, the key number is in the hundreds place. If the hundreds digit is 5 or larger, round up to the nearest thousand. If the hundreds digit is 4 or less, round down to the nearest thousand.

**Examples:**

Round 7,932 to the nearest thousand.
9 is the key digit.
If it is more than 5, round up.
**Answer: 8,000**

Round 1,368 to the nearest thousand.
3 is the key digit.
If it is less than 4, round down.
**Answer: 1,000**

**Directions:** Round these numbers to the nearest thousand.

8,631 — **9,000**       1,248 — **1,000**       798 — **1,000**

999 — **1,000**       6,229 — **6,000**       8,461 — **8,000**

9,654 — **10,000**       4,963 — **5,000**       99,923 — **100,000**

© Carson Dellosa Education — 45

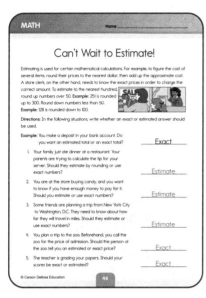

**Page 46**

**Page 47**

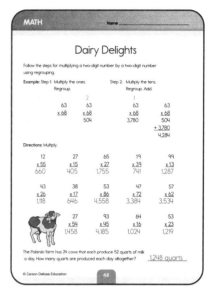

**Page 48**

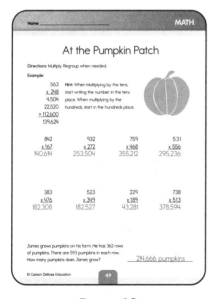

**Page 49**

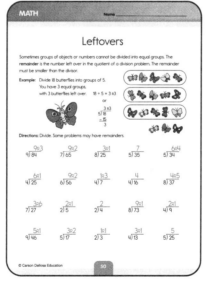

**Page 50**

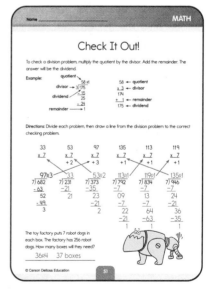

**Page 51**

# ANSWER KEY

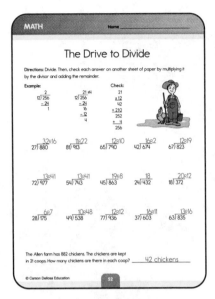

**Page 52**

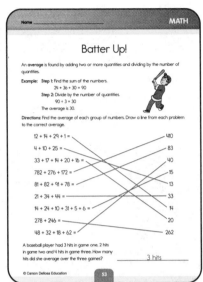

**Page 53**

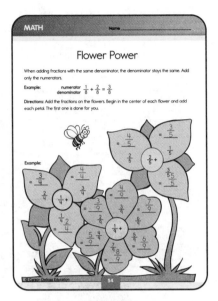

**Page 54**

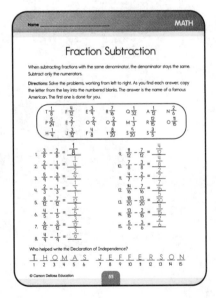

**Page 55**

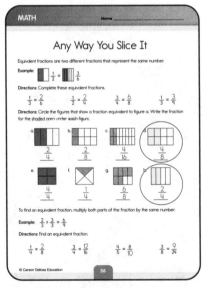

**Page 56**

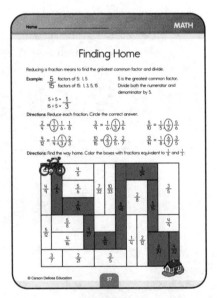

**Page 57**

© Carson Dellosa Education

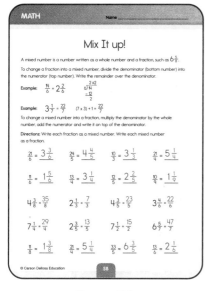

**Page 58**

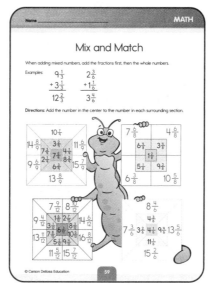

**Page 59**

**Page 60**

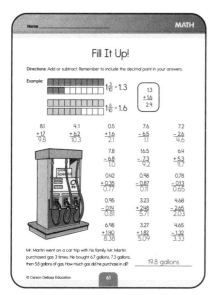

**Page 61**

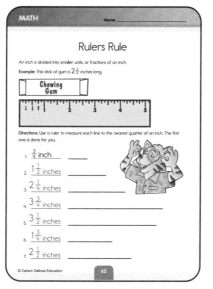

**Page 62**

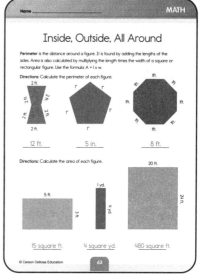

**Page 63**

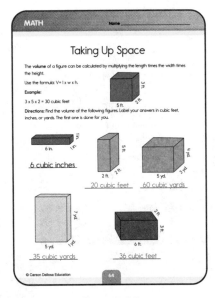

**Page 64**

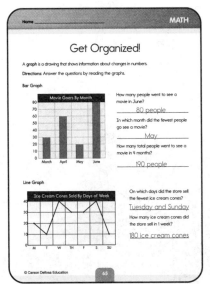

**Page 65**

**Picture a Polygon**

A **polygon** is a closed figure with three or more sides.

Examples:

| triangle | square | rectangle | pentagon | hexagon | octagon |
|---|---|---|---|---|---|
| 3 sides | 4 equal sides | 4 sides | 5 sides | 6 sides | 8 sides |

**Directions:** Identify the polygons.

octagon     rectangle

square     hexagon

pentagon     triangle

**Page 66**

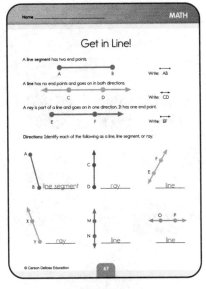

**Page 67**

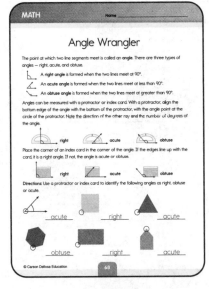

**Page 68**

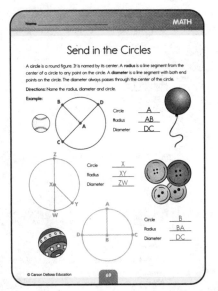

**Page 69**